# Dreaming a New World

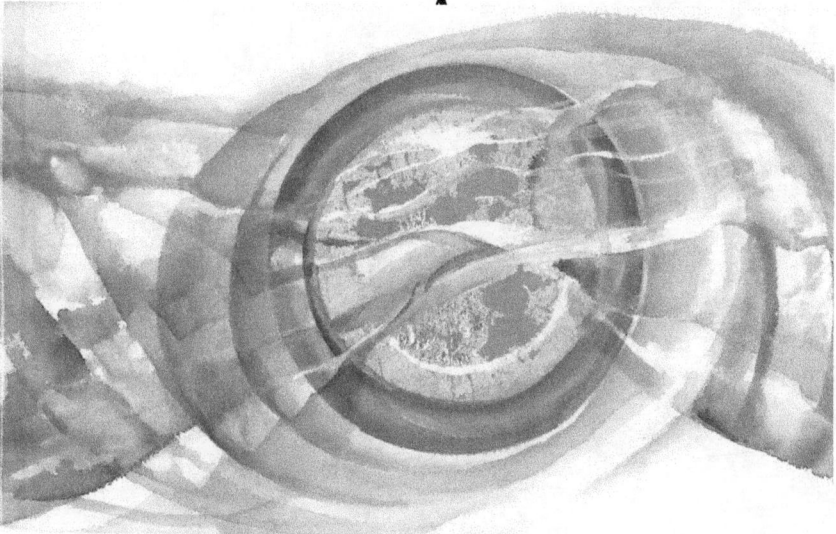

# Dreaming a New World

## A
## Spiritual Journey
## of
## Hope and Transformation

Nancy Van Domelen

In loving memory of our mom, Nancy Van Domelen, and in honor of the wisdom and healing she shared through Dreaming A New World, we, her children, are carrying forward her legacy. With deep respect for her incredible vision, we are sharing her knowledge, insights, and guidance so that the transformative power of her work may continue to touch lives and inspire a fresh generation of readers seeking hope, healing, and a path to a brighter world. Please enjoy and share this updated edition.

Identifiers:
Library of Congress Control Number (LCCN): 2025914069
Paperback ISBN: 978-1-961993-39-6

Color painting used by permission of the artist, Marika Popovits, Crestone, Colorado. This watercolor is called The New Creation and is part of her 12-painting series titled "The Creation Story." Author photo by Colleen Black, Del Norte, Colorado.

I dedicate this book to all those souls who have walked the pathways of Earth down through the ages and to all those who will live on this beautiful planet in the future. Among these beings, there have been some that consciously attuned to the realm of spirit envisioning a better way for all of us. They showed us how to dream and create a New World. For that we shall be eternally grateful.

# TABLE OF CONTENTS

Acknowledgments ................................................... ix

## HOW IT BEGAN ...............................................1

## THE LIGHTBRINGERS ...................................11

## THE PLAN OF CREATION ...........................17
Earth's Purpose • 21
Blueprint of the Almighty • 24
Feminine Principle of the Earth • 25

## A JOURNEY THROUGH TIME ....................29
Motherland of On • 30
The New Human Species • 32
The Role of the Sun and Moon in Early Times • 36
Concept of Monotheism • 38
The Intermediary • 39
Christian Religion and Its Church • 41
Crystallization of Ritual • 45
The Americas, a Cradle of Civilization • 46
United States as Seed Carrier • 49

## A NEW LOOK AT THE HUMAN EXPERIENCE ........53
Desire and Fear • 54
Sin • 55
Worry • 57
Perfectionism • 59
Continuity • 61
Discrimination • 62

Love • 66
Death • 69
Relationships • 71
Sexuality • 84
Addictions • 92

## DEVELOPING PERSONAL POWER .............................97

Functioning in a Transpersonal Capacity • 100
Personal Realization • 102

## THE DIVINE DANCE –
## AN EBB AND FLOW OF ENERGY ..........................107

Attunement • 108
Earth as a Laboratory for Growth • 113
Our Body's Vibratory Field • 115
Triangulation • 117

## THE GREAT AWAKENING –
## A PERIOD OF TRANSITION ..............................123

The Third Dimensional World • 126
A Time of Change • 131
The Millennium • 136
Miasms • 143
Earth's Healing Crisis • 150

## THE WORLD TO COME ...................................161

Love of Self • 163
A Time of Transformation • 166
Universal Frequency Band • 168
The Great Cleansing • 170

# ACKNOWLEDGMENTS

I would like to express my love and appreciation to the following people for the assistance and support that they offered me during the creation of this book:

Rebecca VanDenBerghe who consulted, edited, designed and walked with me throughout the entire process

Genevieve Miller who provided continuous encouragement and loving interest at every step, never allowing me to falter

Lata Shambo who was the midwife that helped birth this creative endeavor by assisting me in grounding and focussing the incoming energies;

Lola McElhaney who contributed her ideas and graphic skills to the book's publishing efforts.

The staff at About Books, Inc. who provided the structure and resources to bring this book into print.

My husband, my children, and my grandchildren who have always loved and accepted me for who I am and have never tried to change that part of me that receives transmissions from the realm of spirit.

# How It Began

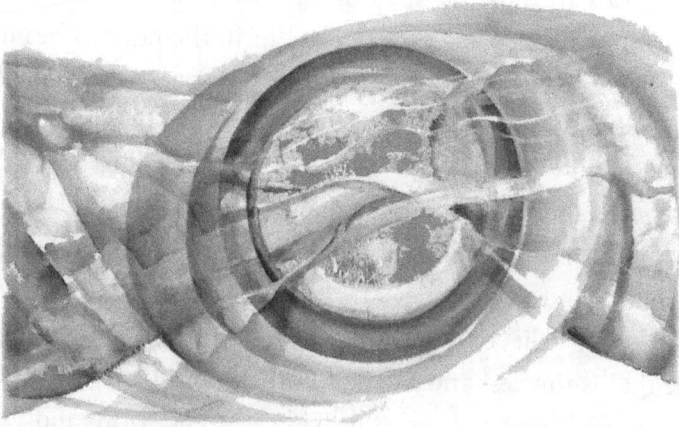

My journey into the realm of spirit began in January of 1973. My husband, two sons and two daughters, and I left the Midwest, where we had lived all of our lives, to move to the mountains of Colorado. We settled in a small town high in the breathtakingly beautiful country of the Western Slope. Little did I know that this move was symbolic of the change in direction my life was going to take. I was beginning the ascent into the higher realms of spirit, just as the cars bringing my family and me were rising from sea level to an elevation of 8,000 feet.

Throughout the next six years, I came into contact with many individuals and books that expanded my awareness and opened me in countless ways to new realms of thought. I sustained an injury skiing, which required that I reduce my activities in all areas of life for some time. I did not realize it then, but this healing respite gave me the opportunity to read and absorb many metaphysical books, which were readily available in my new locale.

As I read, a growing sense of wonder and awe seemed to fill me. When I was a child, I had been deeply religious, attending a parish school for eight years. In my teens, I left organized religion, entering a long period where my values centered on the outer world of matter. Looking back to those days, I can now see what a "dark night of the soul" this time was for me spiritually. But in the rarefied beauty of the mountains, I began to tap into a deeper part of myself that I had forgotten was there.

Then in July of 1979 my youngest son was killed in a mountain climbing accident. The agony of the grief and loss that I experienced seemed to tear me open and shatter my life into a thousand pieces. As I attempted to find a way to heal, I was brought face to face with the issue of what I truly believed. Is there a realm of spirit? Do we all possess an essence that is timeless and exists after the death of the body? Was that being who had been my son still living in some form, and was he all right? Could a mother's love transcend time and space to reach this son, who had left so quickly and violently, to offer support and nurturing, if needed?

These were the questions that absorbed me, and which I felt had to be answered. It was as if a powerful inner force turned me in a new direction and set me on a path, which has continued to this day. Since that time, my life has changed irrevocably. The loss of my son had closed many doors for me and led me in new directions of expansion and personal growth.

One of the most significant developments in my life happened three years after the accident. In a session with a friend who had developed advanced psychic capabilities after her own near-death experience, I received information indicating that it would be in the highest good for me to write after meditating for a brief period of time. I reflected quietly and carefully upon this unexpected information.

Two days later, on the morning of April 1, 1982, I stilled myself and entered into a state of prayerful meditation with pen in hand and a pad of paper on my lap. After some time, to my amazement, I started to write. What came forth was a short letter from my son who had been killed. He expressed his love and said that he was here to help me get started with this endeavor. I was astounded and deeply moved. It then took almost three years of intermittent writings for me to become at ease and to trust this process of connecting to those on the realm of spirit.

Throughout the decade of the 1980s, I received writings on a regular basis from two spirit beings, one purporting to be masculine and the other to be feminine. For a few years, my son would send an occasional letter, but after a while contact with him stopped. The fact that these writings came forth in the form of letters was ironic to me. All of my life I had struggled with the task of writing letters. My solution was to ignore this important area of communication whenever possible. So, for my contact from spirit to occur in the form of a letter was a gentle joke indeed.

My life during these years contained many of the same issues and events that everyone experiences. But throughout all the ups and downs, there were two constants that I could always depend upon — the steady loyalty of my husband and family, and the ongoing contact with my companions from the realm of spirit.

The information that came to me was generally personal, assisting me in areas of self-improvement, in transcending painful times and in seeing the difficulties of life from a higher, more expanded view. It often spoke of the Divine Creator that lives, moves and exists in all of us. The two beings contacting me always expressed love and support in a continuous, ongoing fashion. I came to value this unusual relationship with spirit as a significant part of my life.

Then in the late 1980s, my source of contact with the realm of spirit changed. The two spirit beings that had offered such wise, loving counsel departed and were replaced by what seemed to be a group of souls. The focus of the writings also started to change. My personal growth and development were still considered, but many writings spoke to issues that were broader and more universal in theme. I began to have the feeling that others could truly benefit from what I was receiving, but I had no sense that the process would change.

In 1992, my husband and I made a life move. We left the mountains of western Colorado and relocated to the red rock canyon country of southeastern Utah. The rugged, austere beauty of the land with its hot, dry climate enhanced a deep sense of connection to both the Earth and the plane of spirit. The remoteness and isolation proved very conducive to achieving a balance of body, mind and spirit. And so life flowed on through these early and midyears of the last decade of the century.

Then, in late 1996, a shift of major proportions occurred in my life. I was informed through the writings that it was now time to offer this information to a wider audience. I was asked to make a commitment to receive a body of transmissions that were to be put in book form and published. Again I was at a turning point that required careful thought and consideration on my part. I had spent twenty years in positions of public responsibility and had enjoyed the last thirteen years of peaceful respite away from that arena.

However, I felt great love and appreciation for the spiritual beings that had offered such wise counsel and assistance to me down through the years and a deep excitement about this new information. And so it was that I accepted the request with the intent of doing the best that I could in the unknown process that lay ahead. In June of 1997, the transmissions began in earnest. My personal writings had all been by hand, so the first task was to become proficient on the computer, a machine that had never been very natural to me. But I was told that we were in a new age heavily influenced by technology. And, therefore, the transmissions must be provided through the vehicle that is most widely used in this era.

The group of souls communicating with me identified themselves as the Lightbringers. They said that whenever there is a uniting of the two realms of spirit and matter, it is most significant indeed. Not only is the information brought to the Earth plane beneficial, but also the process is a demonstration of future capabilities that will be common to all. For we are here to learn that human beings are units of physical matter, which house an indwelling essence of All That Is. This inner spirit which we all possess is the true guiding force of our lives and is the means by which those incarnating on Earth can be in continuous contact with the many dimensions of time and space.

The Lightbringers also said that this communication coming from the realm of spirit is meant to assist and uplift a small segment of souls at a key time during the Great Awakening. The individuals who will read the information sent from the Lightbringers have important actions to perform on behalf of the transformation about to occur on planet Earth. They need inspiration to strengthen and enlighten them along the way. They said that these souls have been laboring in the vineyard, as it were, and are in sore need of spiritual rejuvenation. The information provided through the transmissions is meant to uplift and sustain them as they continue their work.

Then my friends in spirit outlined very specifically the process that would be the most conducive to writing this book. I was asked to quiet myself before every transmission and attempt to raise my consciousness to a higher level. They suggested that I visualize myself in their company and in harmony with them. They said that what I would be seeing in my mind's eye would actually be happening on another dimension. All of this personal information was relayed intermittently throughout the course of the transmissions.

Then they made specific suggestions that would be beneficial and support me throughout the period when I would be receiving the transmissions. They indicated that it was very important to establish a rhythm to my life that would enhance this process. Each day needed to flow with beauty and grace, nurturing and supporting me. The early hours of the morning and the quiet lovely periods of the evening would be the most auspicious time for writing.

They recommended above all that I live a simple life, selectively choosing only beneficial family and social interactions. They said that the exercise I enjoyed in gardening, walking and some golf would be helpful. Daily yoga and meditation were mandatory since these practices readjusted the electromagnetic wiring in my body. They indicated that my physical body would change in order to receive the higher voltage vibrational energy that is needed to transmit this information. They asked that I eat foods vital in life force since I would be expending much energy during the transmission process, which would tax me physically. Vitamins, supplements and herbs were suggested also.

My friends spoke about the importance of being in water—hot tub, pool or bath. They said that water soothes and stabilizes the electrical system, refreshing it at a deep level of body, mind and spirit. They reminded me that our bodies are primarily water and require a similar environment for renewal. In addition, the use of flower essences was advised to balance the electrical and nervous systems of my body. Rest, play, and enjoyment of nature completed the loving recommendations they made to assist me in being able to receive the information they would be sending.

Even though my friends in spirit gave many suggestions, each of which was important for the overall effectiveness of the transmission process, I was not always able to follow through as asked. My spirit was willing, but my personal resolve was weak at times. I struggled periodically with self-doubt about my ability to receive, was distracted by many situations arising with family and friends, and also found it difficult to remain on task over an extended period of time. But despite all of these obstacles, somehow I was able to continue with the work they had requested. I saw my role simply as a receiver of information. I recorded it as accurately as possible, altering the content slightly for clarity when needed.

My guides were always loving and supportive, never chastising me for backsliding or being unable to produce as I had been requested. They said that it was most important for me to retain my independence throughout this process, and that I must always honor myself above all else. If what they had asked of me did not seem feasible, I was told that I must follow my own self-wisdom. They indicated that this concept would be emphasized in the coming age as one of its key teachings. It is most important to remain the directors of our own energies and not allow anyone or any group to dictate a course of behavior to us, which does not resonate positively with our inner knowing.

A most intriguing portion of the transmission process was the triangular matrix that the Lightbringers established at the outset of the work. In order for this book to be a true co-creative activity, a joining of the realm of spirit with the realm of matter had to occur. Triangulation of energy would serve as the seedbed and source for the emergence of this information. This particular matrix carries with it the vibrational quality of the emerging times and enhances the ability of those reading this book to receive it a deeper level of spirit.

They asked that I perform a triangular invocation at the beginning of each writing. They told me that three is the most harmonious number in the universe. All that is created occurs within the harmony of the Divine Triangle. Uniting the realm of spirit and Lightbringers with me as receiver and the Earth as a base would enhance the power of the work. And so the first triangulation consisted of the Lightbringers, the Earth and me.

Throughout all of the phases for creating the book, triangular units were established at each important juncture. A friend joined me to establish a triangulation between the two of us and the realm of spirit. Her role throughout the process was to be the grounding element for the work. She was asked to read all of the transmissions, reflecting contextually upon what was being sent from the plane of spirit. This act would begin to anchor the material on the Earth plane. Another friend who had editing skills formed a third triangle with me and my spiritual guides when the refining portion of the work began.

And so the request for a triangular energy matrix was honored throughout each phase of receiving, transcribing, organizing and editing this book. The arranging of the 100 transmissions that had been received in letterform was an experience of deep spiritual significance for me. After meditation and attuning to the realm of spirit, my friend who had grounded the writings and I joined the Lightbringers to create the number of chapters with their titles in a highly energized one-hour session.

Previously, I had identified the key ideas in each transmission. I was asked to prepare myself again and arrange the transmissions within the chapters to which they pertained. Using a pendulum as a visual aid to reflect the wishes of my friends in spirit, I was able to place all of the transmissions in the order found in the book in less than a two-hour period. Without their help and guidance, this process could have taken weeks. This one experience illustrated more strongly to me than any other the enormous advantage one receives when creating in cooperation with spiritual assistance.

(The Lightbringers emphasized from the outset their intent to make the book we were creating together clear, concise and readable. They indicated that there would be a minimal amount of editing required and I was always to honor basic content received from them. Any changes of the transmissions were minor, and I always stayed connected to the Lightbringers for approval. One other person assisted in the primary editing function. She always was in contact with the Lightbringers to assure the changes were acceptable. It was always a wonder to me that such a productive working relationship could be established between the realm of spirit and the human world!)

And so I offer, for the reader's consideration, the fruits of this endeavor. (The remainder of this book consists entirely of one hundred transmissions received from the Lightbringers over a twelve month period.) As my friends in spirit say so well throughout this book, we are moving into wondrous times. Human beings are taking a great step forward up the spiral of life. It is time for us, as residents of this beautiful planet, to lift our heads and awake to the proximity of the world of spirit all about us. We need to see our lives and ourselves with clarity and truth. Only then can we start the process of creating and dreaming a new and better world.

Nancy Van Domelen
July, 1998

# The Lightbringers

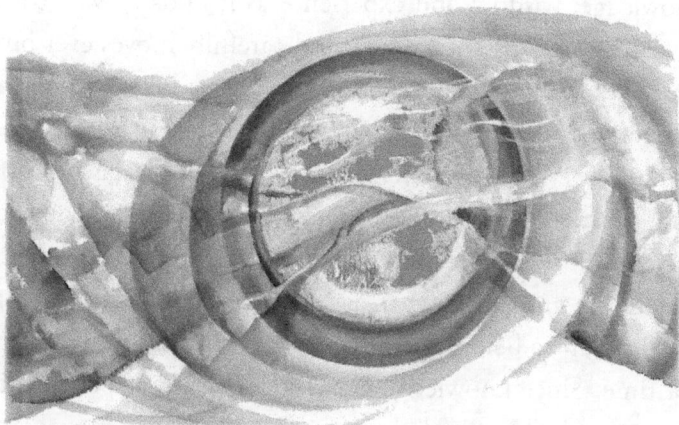

We welcome all of the readers of this book as sisters and brothers in spirit. We call ourselves the Lightbringers since we were created out of the mind of the Godhead. Our purpose is twofold. We bring light in the form of information to any part of the universe activated on behalf of the unfolding of the Divine Plan. We also participate in expansion experiences in an ongoing way as a type of spiritual development program assigned by higher dimensional powers. Our connection with the receiver of these transmissions since 1982 is an example of the continuous contact and maintenance for which we are responsible. You can see evidence of our presence wherever you see enlightenment, expansion and awareness at work.

As many of you read our words, you will start to feel the power emanating from the source of these transmissions. You ask, from whence comes the source of this power? As we have already indicated, we are

11

part of a group soul existing throughout the many universes of time and space. Our primary function is to bring information for illumination and enlightenment. As all souls proceed up the spiral of life, they grow in awareness of who they really are — a spark created at the beginning of a period of manifestation as part of the Prime Creator.

Each spark flows through the fields of spirit and matter acquiring knowledge, wisdom and experience as it finds its way back to the Source. As the soul essence slowly and carefully moves ever onward, it often receives a helping hand either from a great being who brings added awareness, from a peak experience that creates a shift in perception, or from a written source which helps extend the vistas of knowledge. Any one of these experiences supplies the assistance needed to take a step upward on the sacred spiral of life.

We are the group soul that has taken the responsibility for bringing information to beings throughout the universes down through the eons of time. Since knowledge is encoded within a specific vibrational frequency, which emits light, we carry the designation or name of Lightbringers. We are not teachers. We bring information, which is instrumental in raising the vibrational frequency of individuals to a higher state of consciousness.

Once a person's perspective or worldview is heightened, a whole new set of probable futures will present themselves for consideration. So, at the outset of each period of physical manifestation, a given group of souls is assigned the responsibility of expansion, just as other groups are given tasks that assist in the evolutionary plan of life unfolding throughout the universes of the Creator.

The role of Lightbringers is especially significant at this point in time on Earth. Your planet is moving into a powerful energy field which will bring a vibrational impact of major proportions to all those currently living in this part of the galaxy. Periodically, solar systems move into a molecular mass pregnant with stimuli, which provides an evolutionary step forward for those beings in incarnation at the time of the occurrence.

Your planet is completing a great cycle of time — one that only could be comprehended in its entirety by a society like the Mayans, who had perfected the Long Count, a method of computing time into the millions of years. They understood the significance of the various cycles, and how humans on the Earth would be affected by the changes in the subatomic particles infiltrating the atmosphere surrounding the planet. This forcefield has been called the photon band in recent literature. It is an accurate designation, since photonic particles constitute the primary unit of energy making up this vibratory wave.

We, as a group soul, have a specific mission on Earth at this point in time. Our assigned task is to bring to the souls on this planet the information needed by them to raise consciousness. That is all there is to it. Simple, is it not? But it is so sublime at a deeper level of understanding. Information is light, hence the word enlightenment. One can see the importance of new information that changes the view an individual has of the environment in which he or she lives.

New comprehension is truly paradigm shifting in many ways seen and unseen. The shift occurs at the most basic cellular level. As the mind records a new pathway in the brain, the message is sent out to every cell in the body that a new program is being imprinted. When the information is then accepted and a commitment is made on the part of the individual, there is an expansion of the database of the soul.

Existence reduces down to one simple but profound verity. All that exists on the many planes of both spirit and matter reflects gradations of light force. The more a given state is spirit infused, the more light particles there are contained in that state. The diminishing of spirit results in a corresponding reduction of light, causing a density of matter to form, which coalesces into atomic particles of a given weight. This is a fundamental rule that provides the underpinning of the entire process of existence and creation in the universe. So, it is important to recognize that enlightenment exists in each and every person, thing and situation.

Why do we speak now of such an abstract and weighty matter? We do so because this information relates directly to the process of bringing light in the form of new knowledge to a given place at any point in time. We are called the Lightbringers because that is truly what we do. Now you can understand why light found in sunlight has always been important to so many of you reading these words. The rays of the sun, received in moderation, have a powerful rejuvenating effect. There is nothing to fear in accessing the sun's rays, though many believe the opposite is so. So reflect upon these words. We want you to have full and cognizant awareness of what is involved at the fundamental level of energy.

Our mission is to bring light to any place of darkness. This light supplies information, which then brings illumination to the receiver. This process is different than teaching, which implies a direct involvement over a period of time with personal interaction as a prerequisite. Bringing information is a totally different situation. Information, which supplies enlightenment for the receiver, brings an expansion of awareness. Often the source of the information has no direct contact whatsoever with the receiver, and in fact may not even be known by the individual who has been exposed to the new knowledge.

The transmission process will have an underlying theme, which will emerge as we progress. Human beings on planet Earth are transmuting into a new and more advanced species. These beings will possess powers and capabilities far beyond those of the average man and woman of today. The transmissions will speak to these capacities in a clear and recognizable way. The universe, the galaxy and your solar system are experiencing a great step forward on the spiral of life. The transmissions will speak to this expansion process. Many of the human capabilities that have developed down through the eons, as spirit descended into matter and began its evolutionary return to its Source, will be identified in the transmissions.

The transmissions will offer a new view of the human condition, which will be, in essence, a reawakening to what has been known by all since the beginning of time. And finally, in its entirety, this information will be a message of hope and empowerment for all its readers. The knowledge contained within the words will be an imprint activator for those people who read them, which then will release their dormant capabilities for full-fledged expression.

We, the Lightbringers, have served the Divine Plan of the Almighty down through the many ages of human existence on the Earth. Some of us incarnate in human form, while the remainder of us stay in the realm of spirit to serve as contacts and energy transmission forces for fellow group members who require our assistance.

The Pleiades star system currently is our home base, although we operate throughout the many universes of time and space. We have served as inspiration and guidance down through the ages for emerging civilizations. In this role, we have appeared through out the planet to offer a cultural matrix for a wide variety of living experiences. We have not been here consistently but intermittently, when conditions were right for our vibratory essence to penetrate.

Our purpose in the Grand Plan is to anchor the vibration of love and harmony onto the Earth so that human beings can return to the source of Great Spirit. There have been many periods of darkness on the Earth when we did not take part in the activities of the evolutionary plan. We would wait until a more propitious time for us to offer our assistance.

But now we are here in full force, as you would say in your world, to participate in the Great Step Forward that your planet is about to take. We have been intimately connected to the unfolding of the Divine Plan on Earth down through the ages. And so it is with great respect that we join our essence with the many souls in incarnation. These souls are aware, to some degree, of these momentous times and are attuning more and more to the realm of spirit. Welcome! We love you all!

# The Plan of Creation

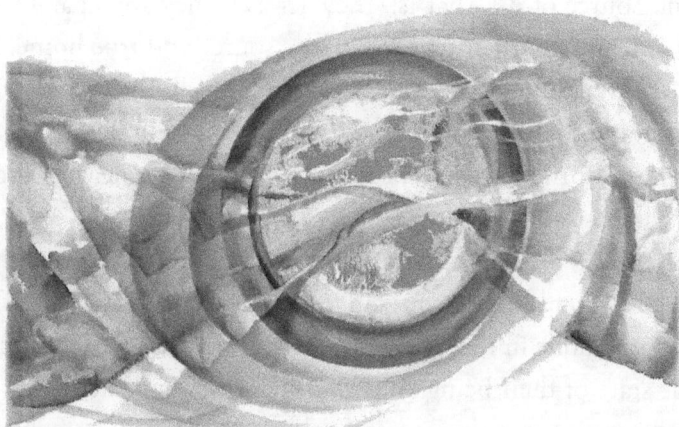

In the beginning, at the creation of this current universe, all was still — a softly undulating wave of Divine Consciousness, unmanifested and serene. Then slowly the One began to emerge into another cycle of creation. This awakening took millions of years in today's system of counting time. The whole purpose for the awakening of the One was the desire to create and experience the manifested state at the level of matter.

The One chooses these periods and their characteristics each time so that a new divine drama can come forth for the Almighty's play of consciousness. It is as if a performance of cosmic proportions unfolds with the theme and development of a prescribed plot or plan. It is now time for those living on the Earth to see themselves in a much broader context than the one they currently use.

Originally all beings were sparks of this divine unmanifested essence residing in an undulating wave. Then they emerged at the bidding of the One to create and experience in the fields of matter. The sparks of the Divine One are always connected to their Source by a golden cord of energy. They also contain a divine essence that is ever attuned to the One for receiving a continuous flow of information and energy.

Most humans at this time do not know of the connection they have with the Source of All That Is. They act as if they are separate, disconnected and alien to their true state, true source and true home. But the period of Awakening is here and many are lifting their heads, opening their eyes and looking about them as if after a long sleep. Many more will awaken in the decades ahead until truly a new heaven and a new Earth will exist on the planet.

This is the theme of the current manifestation in your universe. Souls lose awareness at the human level of who they truly are. They live separate and alone in the fields of matter. Finally they become aware of the true state of their being and why they are living encased in matter. It is at this point that they come forth, spirit-infused, joyfully creating in the divine essence of the Almighty. It is an interesting play, is it not?

The reason we speak of these matters is because it is time for all of you to see yourselves as one of these sparks of the Divine Creator. It is vital that you acknowledge your continuous connection with the Source of All That Is. Know that through your eyes and essence the Almighty experiences what it is to be a spirit living and creating on the different planes of matter found in your universe.

So each day it is of vital importance to connect with the Source through the spiritual practices of meditation, prayer, chanting and receiving. Yes, receiving, because communication between the world of spirit and the world of matter will be stepped up with great intensity. That is why human beings need to become receptive to the messages that will be forthcoming. It also is important to strengthen and tone the body so that it can be a worthy and stable receptor for the divine energies.

The body can be compared to an electrical system found in your homes today which serves as a conduit for 110 and 220 watts of voltage. You know that the wiring and receptacles are different in order to carry the different voltages of power. The analogy is a perfect parallel to your body. The spiritual practices we have mentioned above rewire the physical being so that one can become a conductor of these higher vibrational energies.

Human beings also serve as transmitters from the Divine Source. You are meant to project these spiritual energies onto the Earth as many are learning to do. The entire energy field of the Earth is gradually being healed in this manner, as are the human, plant and animal kingdoms. So see these simple spiritual practices as daily regimens in the wider scheme of expanding human awareness.

The food an individual eats, the thoughts one thinks, the actions one performs are all directed to upgrading one's vibrational frequency. So all of those residing on Earth can truly participate in and assist this play of the Almighty. We ask that each of you reading these words take your responsibility seriously. Achieve the spiritual development for which you have been preparing down through the ages. There is great love and support on the plane of spirit for all of God's children who are toiling in the fields of matter. Take heed to our words. We love you all.

As you read other books, which have been received by those on Earth from the realms of spirit, you see again the great beauty and inspiration they offer. It is the intent of those of us given the responsibility of shepherding this new evolutionary step forward to work closely with those of you who are serving as receivers. We are here with you all, guiding and seeding these thoughts and ideas into the pathways of your brain.

The process manifests as a fusion of two differing realms coming together in a beautiful creative act. This was the intent of the Prime Creator when the most recent plan for the developing universes was formulated. The Idea was to start creation with total unity on all levels of existence. Then a gradual separation would occur which would hide spiritual beings from the knowledge of and connection to their source.

The realm of matter was created to serve as the agent for this removal from spirit. As incarnating souls sunk deeper into physical life, they simply forgot who they were and from whence they had come.

But part of the Plan or Divine Game was to have a certain segment of souls remain in full awareness. They were given the task of assisting and guiding the souls immersed in the fields of matter back into conscious realization. They would accomplish this assignment by bringing information or assistance in the form of teachings presented in different ways.

Many times a teacher of great spiritual power would come and raise consciousness so that those immersed in matter would take a major step forward on the return to their Source. Or ideas would be implanted or channeled so they could be given out at times selected as key in the divine unfolding.

This process still is in effect today. In fact, the overall outline of the divine intent is more and more apparent every day. The infusion of light-encoded subatomic particles is increasing in intensity on a regular basis. But it is important to note that this same activity is occurring everywhere in the many universes of time and space.

Those currently residing on the Earth plane see themselves as alone and isolated within the universe. But nothing could be further from the truth. The esoteric saying "as above, so below" holds a profound truth that is wise to reflect upon. The universes of time and space are teeming with life of many different forms and manifestations. Those living on Earth need to know this truth. Very soon in your manner of counting time, this fact will be evident to everyone existing on your planet.

Those individuals living within the indigenous cultures all over the Earth have been in constant contact with beings from other realms. They have been instructed to start disseminating the information that will open the eyes and minds of earthlings as to their true state. Then key events will happen which will literally blow the circuits of the minds of those who believe that they are the only ones in the universe.

At the same time, there will be more evidence to support the knowledge that numerous beings existing in spirit form have been interacting with those on Earth on a regular and continuous basis.

So you see what an amazing time this is — one filled with adventure and excitement. It is not often that such a major evolutionary step forward occurs. Flow with it, dancing and rejoicing that your lives will be filled with more light and love than you can ever remember. Fill yourselves with a spirit of love, joy and anticipation. You are all here for an astounding event!

The time is upon us for this great evolutionary shift to occur in the universe, your galaxy, and on planet Earth. God is introducing a new vibratory energy into the world of matter — an energy that will expand all molecules at the subatomic level of matter to prepare for the infusion of Divine Grace which will be coming into the Earth plane in these next twenty years. The process is already underway, albeit at a very diminished rate.

At the turn of the century the intensity and rate of infusion increased one hundred fold. So all beings on the Earth plane had a short time to prepare their bodies, minds and spirits for this event. Since the year 2000, the turbulence and psychic distortions have been rough going for inhabitants of the planet. People all over the Earth are totally absorbed in adjusting to and surviving the many changes entering their lives. If they used the few years left before these events appeared for preparation, then they are more able to ride the waves of change with confidence and a sense of well being.

# Earth's Purpose

We now would like to speak regarding the purpose of the Earth in the wider scheme of universal spiritual development. For your beautiful blue-green sphere was created by All That Is for a very specific reason many eons ago. It was determined at the highest levels of this universe that a clearly defined Plan was to be enacted which would serve as the blueprint for this cycle of manifestation. The Plan was simple but very profound in its basic essence. Divine Creator would call into being many different aspects of itself to embark upon a journey far from home and source.

These sparks of spirit had been given a specific task to fulfill. As children of the Creator, they were to fashion many different worlds, each of which would reflect the basic essence of the Godhead. For you see, the quality of this Divine Plan was akin to the Earth game of hide-and-seek. At the core of every created being was the spark of spirit that reflected the Source. But the outer expression was very different.

The goal of the Divine Plan was to bring unity out of diversity. After a long period of time, all those participating would forget who they were and from whence they had come. The children's game of blind man's bluff relates to this divine truth and holds a much deeper significance than has been realized at a conscious level.

In fact, many of the Earth games and stories that are slowly being forgotten contain meanings that kept alive a necessary awareness, which was not recognized for what it really was. Your planet was one of the locations in the universe given the assignment of being a laboratory for the unfolding of this Divine Plan. On Earth, spiritual beings emanating from the Creator were to slowly descend through the many dimensions of time and space into the forcefield of the planet. At a certain point, they would encounter the gravitational pull of the Earth, which would serve as an anchor for them.

At first they were totally conscious of who they were and from whence they had come. But the force of gravity had a sedating effect upon them, causing a gradual loss of memory and awareness. It was at that point that the Divine Game began in earnest. Down through the eons of time as it is measured on Earth, life unfolded on this planet.

The souls residing on Earth needed to experience the qualities of mineral and animal existence as a foundation for human expression.

So for an extremely long period only that type of life existed. But at a certain point, humans of a high level were created to carry on the next phase of the game.

The continents of the planet were different than they are at this time. Suffice it to say it was a world unrecognizable to those living today. But the beings inhabiting the Earth had great beauty and power, which allowed them to live at a high level of personal expression. The first humans were located in one locale and then spread out all over the Earth to seek places suitable for their unfolding.

As their remembrance of whom they were dimmed, rituals and religious practices were established to help them keep some semblance of memory alive. Throughout the long period that followed, as they sank deeper into third dimensional matter, life existed as if through a glass darkly. But about twenty-five centuries ago, Earth was impulsed with universal beams, which slowly started the period of awakening. Great spiritual teachers came to help accelerate the process. They assisted human beings in starting to remember their divine origins.

This brings us now to the significant point in time today. The planet is passing through a dense forcefield of intergalactic photonic particles, which will activate the capabilities of Earth beings greatly. Whereas contact with great teachers was the impetus for expansion in the past, the new stimulus will be provided by contact with beings from other worlds in a concrete and recognizable way.

Many star people have been visiting the Earth since its creation. Stories and descriptions of them can be found all over the planet. But in this time of advanced worldwide technology when they will come and be known for whom they are, the knowledge base of human beings will be expanded greatly. A glow of light will spread all over the Earth, shooting connecting rays out into the farthest reaches of the universe. And planet Earth will instantaneously become an active member of the galaxy — a true partner in the Divine Plan.

So prepare yourselves, our beloved friends on Earth. The time is very close indeed. In a twinkling of an eye the awareness will be upon you, and life will be very different in all ways. Strengthen your physical body so that it can withstand the increased radiation that will be forthcoming. Stabilize your emotional and mental bodies to act as support no matter what the circumstances. And attune to the realms of spirit so that you are always open and receiving whatever information is coming through to you.

All of those currently living on Earth are assisting in the rebirthing process of your planet. What a glorious time to be on the Earth plane! Revel in your participation in this long-awaited galactic event. Those of you who are here for the Great Awakening have worked long and hard on behalf of the Divine Plan. Is not life a wonder of divine proportions?

## Blueprint of the Almighty

A blueprint or plan was established at the very outset of this period of manifestation. It contained the theme or primary issue to be addressed in all the realms of spirit and matter. This current manifestation's theme is the unfolding of love and unity out of diversity and disharmony. It is as simple as that. At the outset of creation, there existed only the very faint outline of the potential form of what was to be. It served as the spiritual blueprint for the goal of this current period of creation. And it is found as the energy background of every type of existence.

For, you see, there always is a divine intent behind every unfolding action, no matter how small or insignificant. This intent is the motivating force in everything that is, whether in the realms of spirit or on the many planes of matter. It is the activating power that emanates from the very center of the Creator and proliferates out in radiant bands of light and energy throughout all the universes of time and space.

Just visualize this concept for a moment. Can you picture a divine center of great power and majesty pulsating and emitting a beat which serves as the energy source for all that is? This description within the limitation of human words defines the nature of the Almighty Godhead.

Much has been written and spoken over the many eons of life on planet Earth in an attempt to describe the properties of God. Nothing can come close to portraying the nature of the Supreme Being since it is unmanifested and therefore unknowable. The Godhead is a mighty force of love, which creates, sustains and dissolves all existing universes. Much of what has been described as God in the various religious literatures upon planet Earth is a description of a being that reflects one or more facets of the Ultimate Unknown, but is not the complete composite of All That Is.

## Feminine Principle of the Earth

The inner turbulence of the Earth, as well as the disharmony of so many of the people throughout the world, is building into a discordant crescendo. Even though there are pockets of serenity and peace, the intensity of the negative areas of war, famine, greed and arrogance is impacting the overall balance and stability of the very planet itself. There are intervals in which the Earth releases the buildup of these energies, almost like a human breathing a deep sigh to relieve inner tension. As many of you become sensitive and aware at a much deeper level, you are able to feel it each time the release occurs.

Also, many of you are becoming attuned and in sync with the rhythms of the planet on which you reside. This capability will increase greatly as the years progress. You truly will become channels for the creative energy of the Divine. So give love to the entity who is the ruling power of your planet. She is in great travail now. She has always nurtured human beings with total love and giving of herself.

We use the feminine designation here because the energy vortex that sustains this physical sphere is a feminine energy construct. Two of the four primary forces are found in great abundance here — water and earth. These two forces are feminine in principle and manifestation. So experience and learning on this planet focuses primarily in the areas of the feminine.

Think about the great civilizations that have grown and prospered on the Earth. They have been imbued with the feminine impulse to grow crops, build homes, create beautiful objects of art and jewelry, and travel the land and seas to connect with others. Great religions have appeared to provide the cornerstone for society. Education of the young has been emphasized in most of the higher functioning cultures.

All of these activities have the imprint of the divine feminine. It is true that there has been war, pillage and rape. But these negative activities form the dark side of the feminine experience. In this realm of duality, there are both positive and negative manifesting simultaneously, providing the crucible for the growth and development of the soul.

One of the capabilities of the feminine principle is the capacity to readjust in times of great need. The masculine principle supplies the opposite strength, the ability to continue on in times of great stress and tension without wavering. These two characteristics are complementary despite their apparent contradictions. Feminine energy senses, intuits and realizes at a deep level when there is an imbalance that must be corrected. It then is able to adjust to a new and more beneficial level. The masculine counterpart continues moving down the road toward the necessary goal.

The only conflict or dissension that can arise in this instance is when the masculine attempts to maintain the position held before the adjustment occurred. It is therefore imperative that the masculine energy recognizes the power of the feminine to navigate the course, as it were. And the feminine must allow the masculine to steer at the helm in order to cross the sea of life.

We ask that all who read these words reflect upon them at length. At this point in time, there is a great misunderstanding about the primary roles of men and women, which is causing pain and suffering on many levels. It is imperative that men and women recognize and honor their primary functions. By that we mean that women need to give men the freedom to perform. And men must accept the capacity that women have for continually sensing, intuiting and adjusting. This awareness is going to be essential for surviving the end years of this age.

Women will serve as the channels for information from higher realms and the connection to the very planet itself as the Earth prepares for its great realignme     nt. Men will offer the strength and power to steer a positive course to safety and survival. That is the main reason there has been such an emphasis on male and female interpersonal relationships in the past twenty years. It has been an intense training course to prepare men and women for the essential roles within partnership, which they will be asked to play in the immediate future.

In the demanding times ahead, the skills and abilities of both men and women acting in concert will be essential for survival. The power struggles, emotional pain, rejection and isolation that are found in so many relationships today must be deemed unacceptable. Couples need to form their unions with love and respect operating at all times. Only the relationships based on these two fundamental primary principles will endure. This is why there seems to be such difficulty sustaining a relationship in this day and age.

The old practical tribal and societal reasons for male-female relationships no longer apply. If mutual love and respect is not the primary operative force in a relationship today, it will split apart because of the centrifugal force of the energy matrix. The powers of the universe know what is needed in the years ahead and are bombarding the planet with the appropriate energy field for success. All truly has been and will be in divine order.

# A Journey Through Time

Back in the early dawn of time on this planet, the beings who inhabited Earth were closely aligned with their spiritual source. They knew clearly who they were and from whence they came. Their inner attuning mechanism was highly developed so that all of their perceptions were clear and illuminated by the divine light of the Godhead. These beings were able to perform and accomplish what today would be considered great deeds. In the cultures throughout the Earth, stories of these people are told in myth and legend. These times were called the Golden Age of the Gods. Ever since, people on the Earth have recalled with longing these periods when life was gentle, beautiful and in harmony with spirit on all levels.

The primary characteristic of what could be considered a paradise-like existence was the close connection that existed with the realm of spirit and the many beings that resided on its various dimensional levels. As the centuries passed and incarnating souls settled deeper and deeper into the gravitational forcefield of the Earth, the connection with the planes of spirit became less powerful. At a certain point in time, those souls on the Earth had forgotten their source and lived as if looking through a glass darkly.

# Motherland of On

So let us look back for a moment at what has transpired on the Earth plane during the incubation and birthing process. As your planet was solidifying and hardening into a denser state, many souls from higher realms were called to take up the assignment of populating the Earth once physical conditions had reached a point that would be receptive for human habitation. This process intensified two million years ago. It took many eons for the incoming souls to become solid enough in form to live within the vibrational forcefield of the Earth. There were many trials and errors, as you would call them, before the physical vehicles were able to exist and prosper in the third-dimensional energy field.

When it was time for the birth of the first great civilization that would be the matrix for all those to come in the future, many souls gathered around the southern pole of the planet, moving into bodies that were prepared for their essences. A great and beautiful land existed in the area that is now called Antarctica. This spot was chosen to house the incoming souls and provide the physical environment for their life expression.

The location of this landmass was more to the north than it is today. The climate was warm, moist, and somewhat jungle-like. It was a land of great natural beauty with days and nights of equal length, which reflected the balance and harmony of the incarnating souls from the higher realms. This land was the true motherland of Earth. All of the primary cultural beliefs and practices originated in this land and then, at a much later time, spread throughout the planet to seed the other peoples who were to begin their journey in matter. This land was called On as it would be understood in your language today. It was truly a Garden of Eden. It served for thousands of years as Earth's cradle of civilization.

Great buildings were erected in honor of the one God, the Divine Source of the Universe. The people lived simple existences in harmony with each other and the forces of nature, which were there for the asking. The law of manifestation, which operated with continuous abundance, supplied every want. Birth was painless and an event of great joy. Death as we know it did not exist. If a soul's time on the Earth plane were ended, gratitude was expressed to the physical vehicle and consciousness was removed to a higher realm. All was in divine order all of the time. Now, those living on the Earth are ready to remember the gifts of the spirit, which were a part of their basic makeup to be used as a reflection of the Creator.

This culture of On was truly the mother for all those that followed. It was the prototype for the many diverse civilizations that appeared in later times on Earth. All the basic elements of human learning originated in this locale — spiritual principles, societal mores, economic, social and political patterns of living, agriculture, and architectural forms later found all over the globe.

After the destruction of On, caused by a massive shift of the Earth on its polar axis, the next great civilizations to emerge were those currently called Lemuria and Atlantis. Continents located in the Pacific and Atlantic Oceans served as the seedbeds for these great and enduring cultures that flourished for many thousands of years. Souls incarnating into these cultures were able to grow in their awareness of what it was to spiritualize matter, which is the primary purpose for incarnating on this planet.

Earth is a great three-dimensional laboratory, providing a setting for souls from higher dimensions who are learning to create in physical form. This concept is most important to grasp. We would like to repeat it again. The primary purpose of existence on this plane is to learn to create in the realm of physical matter. If humans honored this idea, their lives would be very different indeed.

# The New Human Species

Now we would like to speak with you regarding the new species that is in the process of being birthed on your planet. Throughout the history of the development of humans on Earth, there have been key junctures when a great evolutionary step forward has occurred. What is most confusing to your current picture of earlier times is the discovery of the remains of primitive hominid beings. The assumption that they were part of the pattern of human growth and development is in error.

These entities were just a different type of being that peopled the Earth and was not a part of the group of souls known as Homo sapiens. The theory of evolution has been a red herring thrown in to cover the trail of information about the true origins of humankind. Since the beginning of existence on this planet, there have been individuals of great advancement who have lived and established their imprint on the course of human development. While it is true that there is an upward spiral of progress back to the Godhead, it is not true that it started with the most primitive unit of form.

Each major development in the growth of a new species has been accompanied by a distinct civilization with its own continent for self-expression. These races with their corresponding branches within the human family have served as the true tree of life that has grown and encircled the Earth. Preparation is now being made by the great souls guiding the divine plan on Earth to establish the beginning of a new kind of human. The seed place for this being has been the American continent. New principles of individual freedom, respect for law, democratic government, and rights for the lowly and oppressed form the political cornerstone for this new species. It is only in a setting free from oppression and tyranny that human beings can develop greater personal powers.

The Earth is emerging from a long period of growth and development, which could best be characterized by the term expansion. Since the 1500s, in your method of counting, there has been energy of movement and change circulating around the globe which has motivated explorers and pioneers to great feats of heroic activity. Even though the accompanying consciousness of these individuals was more primitive in scope, the purpose of opening up whole areas of the Earth was accomplished in a relatively short period of time.

There occurred a cross-pollination of cultures that would be the precursor to an eventual worldwide civilization, which will be evident by the 22$^{nd}$ century after the birth of Christ. So even though the actions of explorers were counter to the principles of love and respect, they accomplished an important practical function. They brought many different peoples in contact with each other so that they could learn and grow, often in new geographic settings. This preparation was needed in order for a matrix to be in place for the emergence of a new species to occupy the Earth.

For this new species will be mighty indeed. Physically they will be strong with bodies of great beauty. They will possess health at a level not to be imagined at this time. They will also know how to heal themselves by activating their own inner powers. Their connection with the Godhead will be open and operational at all times. They will be able to see the past and future simultaneously, for time will be understood for what it truly is — a field of the Now in which all is contained in its entirety. They will know how to create whatever they need immediately by using the Law of Manifestation. Therefore, lack or scarcity will no longer be a part of the human condition.

But the single greatest characteristic of this new species will be their frame of reference. They always will operate out of a sense of love and respect for their fellow humans, the Earth and all the animals living therein. This is not to say that there will not be an occasional being who reflects the old ways. But there will be few, because the great Purification, which will occur soon, will remove from Earth all those souls who are not operating at the vibrational level needed for the new species. Is it not uplifting to know that this evolutionary step forward is to occur on planet Earth in the future? Always keep your faith and hope alive, knowing that what is occurring in your life is contributing to the overall development and well being of those that will come after you.

Certain individuals are asked to perform the service of transmitting information from the realm of spirit at specifically designated intervals. Their knowing of the task assigned to them is activated at an appropriate time for the unfolding of the Divine Plan. The information-bringing process moves in this manner due to the flow of the vibratory waves that undulate throughout the many universes of time and space.

There is continuous movement as the subatomic particles waft like a river of light in and out of all of creation. If one were to see them at the refined level of sight that is required, it would look like a river of luminous matter ever the same, ever beautiful. But the sparks of light are new, always changing, even though they appear static.

From a higher vantagepoint, all appears as a picture of unbelievable beauty. But within this picture there is diversity and constant change. It is a scene of great significance upon which the soul encased in matter can reflect and meditate. Absorbing this universal river of light into one's very being will activate the unconnected DNA helixes, which make multidimensional functioning possible. It is now time to reactivate the powers which have been the human birthright since the time of creation.

The human species has not been evolving upward in an ever-increasing procession of complexity. On the contrary, primeval beings on this planet had great powers and abilities far beyond what is evidenced today. They had full capacity of their brains, utilizing the entire twelve-helix capability for which they were created. Functioning at this level, they were able to communicate multidimensionally with ease. They were well versed in the Law of Manifestation and could create whatever they needed at any given time. They could teleport their bodies throughout the universe without the aid of physical vehicles. Their powers to create were highly advanced, even for this age of high technology. Remnants of their abilities are told in myth and legend and found in a few isolated places on the Earth. The prime example of their skills is the Great Pyramid in Egypt, which could not be duplicated today with modern engineering knowledge.

So the new species which is emerging will be reactivating a model of humanity which was in existence in earliest times on this planet. Their advanced capabilities were lessened and diminished as they settled deeper and deeper into matter. They lost their vibratory contact with the dimensions of spirit. Gradually their higher sensing mechanisms shut down, creating humans that were separate and earthbound. Other beings from elsewhere in the galaxy assisted in this process as part of the Divine Plan. A scenario of domination and control has been presented as the reason for the lost powers, but at a higher level all was in perfect order in the divine scheme of things.

So reflect upon these words at length. They hold great significance. Bring into memory the knowledge of who and what your species really was in the Divine Plan. Incorporating this knowing at a deep level of being will start to reconnect the dormant DNA helixes, which will reactivate the powers of old. The first indication that this change is occurring will be in the sense of sight. Those humans evolving the pattern for the new species will begin to develop advanced viewing capabilities. They will be able to see at a more refined molecular level. Auras around humans, animals and plants will be instantly observed for what they are. They will be able to recognize the electrical patterns of weather conditions. They will even be able to see the quality of the thought patterns, which those about them are projecting.

As more humans on the planet begin to awaken and remember who they are, a new heaven and a new Earth will sprout from the humus of the Old World of form and matter. So think of this time, so dark to many, as a time of great rejoicing. The sleeping beauty of humanity has been kissed by her divine lover and is awakening to live in harmony and balance within the many universes of time and space.

# The Role of the Sun and Moon in Early Times

Spiritual energies are at their strongest in the time of the full moon. Each cycle of the moon provides an unfolding of some aspect of the Divine Plan in small incremental steps.  A specific and identifiable quality or essence manifests during each phase of the moon. In ancient times, certain cultures brought this knowledge to their people through practices and rituals, which honored and attuned to the energy emanations of the moon.  This was particularly so in those cultures which worshipped the Divine Feminine in all of her various guises. For they knew that the moon was the physical manifestation of a great spiritual being who had accompanied their journey as mother, teacher, lover and friend.

In earliest times, groups of peoples all over the Earth watched the moon in the heavens and planned the important areas of their lives in relationship to the phase that the moon was currently displaying. They knew at a deep level of being that the moon played a significant role in the unfolding of their daily lives. They watched closely the differences found in the ebb and flow of the tides and correlated that knowledge to the affairs of human beings. They came to recognize that the phase of the moon played a significant role in all aspects of agriculture. Planting began to be regulated in relationship to the times of the year and the phases of the moon. They eventually became aware that certain crops needed to be planted at the most advantageous time of the moon cycle for greatest yield.

Calendars were created to reflect the body of knowledge that grew up around all aspects of the moon's appearance in the heavens. These calendars were based solely upon the phases of the moon arranged in chronological order throughout a given year. The months were counted by the amount of time that it took the moon to complete one cycle of new, to full, to new moon again. Each month was the same in length, with a specified number of days at the end of the year for purification and worship. Every moon cycle was given a name that reflected the time of year and the type of activities conducted. The beauty of this system of counting time was that there was a balance created in the affairs of humans that was in harmony with the energy pulsation of the Earth itself.

Those living within the nurturing embrace of the moon's vibrational forcefield felt a sense of security at a deep level of being. Peace and stability permeated all areas of their lives, bringing harmony and balance on an ongoing basis. There was a gentle but clearly felt rhythm sustaining them and offering a strong foundation for their daily activities. People living within this lunar system seemed to flow with a flexibility and grace that reflected clearly their connection to the Feminine Principle.

When the lunar system of counting time was no longer used and calendars came into existence based on the movement of the sun through the heavens, a totally different type of energy impulsed life on the planet. The expression of the Male Principle came into ascendancy. And this was just as it was meant to be in the unfolding of the Divine Plan. The current universe is founded upon the principle of duality in all of its many forms.

For any given period of time, a certain type of human experience will manifest. Then the Great Primary Forces of the universe will shift gears, and the opposite representation will come into being. This is the profound truth held within the Hindu dance of the Lord Shiva. For all of life in the universe could be compared to a slow-moving, rhythmic dance of cosmic proportions. And the generating force of the music is the Prime Creator of All That Is.

So we ask that you who are reading these words to reflect upon them at length. Honor the divine expression of both the male and the female principle. See them for what they are, dual energies which must join together to create wholeness. For the underlying purpose of this current universal expression is to create unity out of diversity which will then ultimately join us with our Creator.

Realize at a deep level of knowing that both the male and female archetype have great beauty and power which together reflects all that exists within the many universes of time and space. Each human being is meant to develop within its soul essence the complete qualities of both the masculine and the feminine. When this finally occurs, there will be a gentle but perceptible sigh of cosmic proportions. All of creation will settle into a long-awaited sleep, to be awakened at some time in the future for a new play of consciousness within the many worlds of the Divine Creator.

# Concept of Monotheism

We ask that you look with the clear eye of spirit at the concept of monotheism — the belief that there is a Primary Being who enters the affairs of humans to assist them, but only if there is loyalty and commitment to that God. There are flaws in this idea, particularly in the personalization of God. It is true, as we have just pointed out, that there is one energy force that exists throughout all of the universes. The Yoga concept of the Shakti comes the closest to expressing accurately the qualities of this force — mind, creativity, will and love.

The central condensation of this force into a point of great power cannot be known or defined in any way but abstractly. This force of mind and creativity forms universes, galaxies, solar systems and all kinds of matter from its own essence. The actual physical or spiritual beings that are created from this force only represent a facet of the whole and can never be seen as the ultimate source of the Godhead.

There has been a grave distortion on the part of most religious beliefs that have arisen on the planet. We now ask that people of Earth recognize the reality and basis for what they have followed in their religions. Much of the warfare and cruelty that has existed can be traced to these flawed beliefs. In the next twenty years the foundations of many religions will be struck down, mainly by discoveries that will show clearly the falseness of these beliefs.

What is needed here is a return to the simple, loving posture of the earliest days on Earth where souls played in the sea of the Holy Spirit — at one and co-creating with the Divine Source, worlds upon worlds upon worlds. It was an age of simple, pure peace and love. Now it is the time to reclaim the primeval state so basic to the Universal Plan. We ask all who read these words to prepare for the revelations that are to come and the ensuing destruction of societal institutions that will occur.

Know that all that happens is for the highest good and therefore feel no fear. The Plan or Blueprint of the Almighty is simply unfolding in its own right and perfect way. All that happened before and all that is to come are in divine order, no matter how it appears in its outward form. Out of diversity and disharmony will come love and unity. For the Great Power of All That Is has mandated this theme, and so it will be.

# The Intermediary

There are words and ideas that must be written and spoken in order for humans on the Earth to consider them. Much of what is believed to be the cornerstone of religious and philosophical thought is in error and seen as if through a clouded lens. These ideas served a purpose wherein a construct was created which became the foundation in which civilizations developed and experienced a frame of reference for incarnation.

These religious and philosophical ideas have formed a frequency of illusion for human experimentation. But now these societal beliefs need to be released so that a new structure can be created - one that will represent the coming step in the turn of the divine spiral. One of the ideas that has been a cornerstone for the past five thousand years centers around the concept of the need for an intermediary between God and man.

Many religions have originated through an evolved being whose teachings have contained essences of liberation and enlightenment. But most of these teachings have been distorted, ritualized and institutionalized by groups who wanted to establish power and control over other beings. They used the most effective and time-honored way to do this. They appealed to a universal awareness found within everyone, which knows that there is a Divine Creator that exists and can be accessed instantly at all times.

The empowerment, which comes with this knowledge, brings all souls into a co-creational relationship with that ultimate Being. It is a basic right for all that exists within the fields of matter. No individual needs the assistance of anyone else to access instantly that Divine Force. But over the eons, many religious structures were created replete with hierarchies, dogma, sacraments and priesthoods. The basic premise was put forth that only through these means could an individual access the love and power of the Divine.

Nothing could be further from the truth. It has really been a gigantic scam that has caused universal pain — the pain of separation from the essence that sustains and uplifts us all. These practices and the entire idea that has created religions with hierarchies, which are given the responsibility of perpetuating them, will be rent asunder in the decades ahead. In the years ahead, much of what has been the foundation for religions will be struck down — mainly by discoveries that will show clearly the falseness inherent in their teachings.

What people will be left with is the pure, simple awareness that they are imbued with the Divine Essence of the Creator — that their primary function is to love and create, whether it be in the realms of spirit or on the many planes of matter. They will come to know that they possess this power and capability to experience great and wondrous things through an ongoing connection with the Source of All That Is. That is all there is — so simple yet so sublime.

# Christian Religion and Its Church

Many efforts are coming forth at this time from various individuals covering different elements of basic spiritual truths. It is a period in the progress of the human being on the Earth where an extensive seeding effort is being enacted to supply the new knowledge base and vibrational encoding for the coming age of development. This new period will be very different from the two- thousand-year cycle that is now ending. Astrological terms are used to define these periods, which is as good a way as any to identify the archetypal human experience emerging during these times.

The Age of Pisces, which has been in effect since the time of the Christ to the end of this current century, has been an era of emphasis on spiritual and religious ideals with their corresponding manifestation into physical reality. The emergence and establishment of Christianity, Buddhism and Islam have formed the religious triad of belief and practice for the western, near eastern and far eastern world. The great challenge down through the centuries has been the task of forming a structure, which stayed true to the actual teachings of the individual upon whom the religion was founded. It has always been thus. For the disintegration process is implicit within each cycle of religious manifestation.

The Christian religion is a prime example of the vast difference between the teachings of a great spiritual leader and the practices, which were established by the followers. Jesus the Christ was a great teacher who came to this planet to uplift the human race into a higher form of functioning. His basic message was simple but so profound. He stated it very succinctly. Love the Divine Creator, love all people, and love yourself. He was the first teacher to distill the myriad of previous religious teachings into one primary essence, that of love. It was time for those on Earth to address the foremost function of all beings — to love. Those who tried to prevent the dispersion of this concept on a wider basis met his message of love for all with its polar opposite, hate.

But Jesus had planted the seed, and love, the greatest power in the

41

universe, spread throughout the world in the centuries after his death. At a deep soul level those in physical incarnation know that the primary purpose for all that lives is to love, create and experience. So each person who heard the message of Jesus was immediately imprinted at a deep level of being and changed even though outwardly it might not have been evident. But it is always thus in the ways of humans that there is a need to prescribe, quantify, limit and control great ideas so they fit comfortably within the current societal matrix of the times.

This is exactly what happened to the great teachings of Jesus. When the Roman Empire adopted the Christian religion under the rule of the emperor Constantine, the current political structure settled over the shimmering beauty of the teachings. Slowly and inexorably, the force and vibrational integrity of the great spiritual message was diminished. And, in fact, the polar opposite of the message of Jesus came into being. Instead of loving God and therefore respecting all expressions of worship by other faiths, the Christian Church took as its primary duty the stamping out of any religious practice that was not approved by the hierarchy of the church.

A second effort and thrust was initiated to seek out and destroy any heretical beliefs or practices that existed within the church. A rigid dogma became the rule of the day for centuries. In order to enforce this dogma, the Inquisition was established to clear the Christian Church of all whose beliefs were different than the current established precepts. The Inquisition was an enforcement arm of the Church, run by priests. It spread throughout Europe, establishing a reign of terror for over six hundred years. Thousands of people from all walks of life were tortured and burned at the stake in the name of the love of Jesus. Jesus taught us to love our neighbor; and yet the church established in his name tortured and killed — the antithesis of the act of love.

It is universal law that what is sent out returns. This powerful and wealthy church which has existed for centuries has a fatal flaw at its core which will bring it down and in the not-so-distant future. No organization or group can manifest the dark side of truth and endure. It is incumbent upon the Christian Church to acknowledge the crimes it has committed against humanity and humbly ask for forgiveness. This church has become a bastion of wealth and power, largely eschewing the teachings of Jesus, which called for the simple goal of loving and serving God, neighbor and self. The wheel of destiny grinds slowly but inexorably onward. The primary goal of life is to unfold basic goodness throughout the many universes of time and space. Goodness, truth and love are the cornerstones of existence. They and they alone are the essence of what will endure.

A breakdown eventually occurs when humans set up religious organizations. There is an immediate limitation that is placed upon the great spiritual ideas of the founder. There are many dimensions in the universes of the Creator. This is what Jesus meant when he told his disciples that in his Father's house there were many mansions. Each dimension has a designated purpose and function in the unfolding of the Divine Plan. And within each dimension there are many beings that have the responsibility for carrying out the activities assigned to them.

The eighth dimension for those on the Earth plane is that of hierarchical power and structure. All beings from the other dimensions have representation in the meetings that are held regularly at this level to decide courses of action that must be taken throughout the many universes of the Creator. The political structure of the United States closely resembles that of the eighth dimension which has served as its prototype. There exists on the realm of spirit an archetypal blueprint for everything that manifests in matter. The great challenge for anything that is created physically in the third dimension is to hold to the truth and goodness of its model. The primary goal of the third dimension is to become irradiated with enough spiritual vibration to maintain the integrity of that which created it.

The Christian Church, in its infancy, began to fall away from the spiritual teachings of Jesus. And as the centuries passed, it became evident that the true essence of the message of love would not be the cornerstone for this church. Great sadness was felt on the eighth-dimensional level, for there were high hopes that the power of the teachings would uphold those who had the responsibility for dissemination. It was not to be, but much was learned in the centuries during the ascendancy of the Christian Church that would be of benefit to the age that will follow. For, you see, entities can learn through positive or negative manifestation of any experience. That is the concept of free will, which was the Creator's gift. There is always the choice. Only when every being that exists throughout all of the universes of time and space chooses the good, will the play of the divine be ended for this cycle.

In the coming age, which has been called Aquarian, much that was experienced during the past two thousand years will sink into the soul knowledge of those who live in the future. They will truly know at a deep level of their being what pain and suffering occurs when one gives his or her personal power over to a hierarchical organization of any kind. They will know that they have a direct contact with the Creator as well as any other realm of spirit they desire. They simply will not support or will walk away peacefully from anyone or group that try to control them. Since no energy will be given to the old model, all religious, political, economic, social, or educational organizations that operate out of control, fear or domination will be unable to sustain themselves for any extended period of time.

There will be growing numbers of humans who will be living and interacting at a higher vibrational level — that of love and respect for themselves and each other. As each individual makes the transition up the evolutionary spiral, more and more light will shine on planet Earth uplifting all that exists. So we say to each one of you: the single greatest service you can offer is the increasing of your own level of vibration through uplifting the quality of your thoughts and actions. The impact it will have on yourself, those about you, and the very Earth itself is far greater than you can ever imagine. The souls coming to the Earth in the coming age will know this truth and will follow it. Then there will be a new heaven and a new Earth, which will radiate out a steady, continuous beat of divine love, impulsing the very universe with its beauty.

# Crystallization of Ritual

Human nature has a strong need for security and control at all levels. It is part of the human genetic pattern imprinted by the Creator. These qualities are a necessary requirement for survival on the Earth plane. But they are also two of the greatest hurdles which humans need to overcome in order to move up the spiral of life. As one reviews the many cultures that have flourished in the past, it can be seen that the religious rituals established by each group soon developed into crystallized forms followed by rote without an accurate reflection of the Holy Spirit.

Certain individuals assumed the power and responsibility for creating and maintaining the practices, which the remainder of the group had to follow. Penalties for disobedience came into being even unto the very loss of life for any deviation from the norm. It has been ever so on Earth since humans developed into the current species inhabiting the planet. We are speaking of this matter because it is now time for those incarnating in human form to move into an entirely new way of connecting with the divine forces of the universe.

Attunement to the realm of spirit and the Creator is now to come in a direct and simple way from the heart and soul of each living person. Ritual and form will no longer be needed once this state of union is reached. Until then, it is true that it helps to follow an established guide for stability and direction in spiritual and religious practices. However, we encourage you not to set up any formalized ritual or emphasis on the sources of these transmissions.

Once names are used and a definitive practice is established, the human propensity for crystallization is set into motion. Control mechanisms come into play, stifling the ability to connect directly to the Source of All That Is. You will notice that many different terms have been used in these transmissions to identify the Godhead. The reason for this is found in the information we are relaying to you at this moment. So much of the pain and suffering of the past has been caused by humans trying to force others into rigid religious rituals and practices, one of them being the proper name for the Supreme Being.

So we would offer a new way for those of you who are reading these words. Do all that you must to reach the state where you know that you are a spiritual entity living within the matrix of the Divine Creator. Focus primarily on this knowing and work diligently to connect in a simple but powerful way with all the many realms of spirit. Use your feelings to inform you when that connection has been made. Develop a firm trust in the knowing of who you are and why you are here. Live simply and joyfully, flowing in a positive way through all of life on this planet. Know also that you are a great and glorious being imbued with the ability to love and create throughout the many universes of time and space.

## The Americas, a Cradle of Civilization

We would now like to speak about the course of history as it has unfolded upon your planet in the Western Hemisphere. There is a blank page in the story of the human race upon planet Earth. The omissions concerning the peoples of the West are so extensive that they almost can be compared to the dark side of the moon, which is unseen and unknown to all inhabitants of the Earth plane. For there is a huge segment of information about the unfolding of the life story of humanity which is virtually untapped in the concrete knowledge base of written history.

In the past sixty years or so, discoveries in the Americas have begun to uncover the extensive heritage of human growth and development in North, Central and South America. The current accepted view of mainstream history and anthropology regarding this area of the Earth is erroneous and incomplete. This view provides an account of the progress of human life that hides the true richness and significance of the history of these peoples and cultures which added so much to the unfolding of the Divine Plan on Earth.

Currently there is no accurate and complete picture of the inhabitants of the planet in regards to who they truly are and from whence they came. Once this history is complete, an expansion of consciousness of major proportions will occur. And so it is at this time that we choose to speak with you about the Americas—that great and fertile matrix for the unfolding of the human story.

One misconception that must be rethought is the popularly held idea that the western continents have been virtually unpopulated until the most recent times. The accepted view of historians has been that people came into these virgin lands through only one means, that of a land bridge between Siberia and the land now known as Alaska. While it is true that this was one route chosen by the ancient ones, it was used in a limited fashion by wandering tribes living in the far northern reaches in earlier times.

Very few cultures of any renown lived in these northern regions of the Earth except an early one located in the Gobi Desert. Most of the great civilizations of ancient times were located within a latitudinal belt of twenty to twenty-five degrees in what is now called the temperate climate zone. The two greatest cultures to arise after the destruction of the motherland of On were Atlantis and Lemuria, as they are currently called. They both grew and prospered in separate continents, one in the Atlantic Ocean and one in the Pacific Ocean.

These two great centers of ancient civilization peopled the Earth with colonies that grew into the cultures of which much has been written in your ancient texts. Major regions for the settlement of new groups were the river valleys of the Nile, the Tigris and Euphrates, the Indus and the Danube. It is currently not recognized, however, that these early cultures had highly skilled seamen who sailed all the oceans of the world in large and sturdy crafts. No area of the Earth was unknown or unexplored by these intrepid sailors. All of the oceans, even those in the far north, were charted with maps of great accuracy, readily available for each voyage.

The continents and landmasses were very different than they are today. Oceans existed where there is now dry land, with settlement found all over the Earth in places now covered by water. Since the Earth shifts periodically in order to correct and adjust the declination of its axis, the habitable land on the planet changes. This process in the Divine Plan is provided in order to insure a rest and renewal cycle, not only for the land itself, but also to offer new areas for emerging peoples and their cultures.

The ancient world was teeming with peoples of different colors and backgrounds who traveled by foot, boat and airplane to every corner of the Earth. The readers of these words may be incredulous regarding the use of aircraft by the early ones. But many of the ancient legends and scriptures speak of beings that traveled by air for transportation and warfare. The Hindu Puranas are just one source where many references can be found about air travel of all kinds.

With the sophistication and expertise that existed in the ancient world, it was an easy matter to explore and settle the Western Hemisphere. And it happened continually, particularly during periods of major Earth changes. To continue to celebrate Christopher Columbus as the first person to find the Americas is a mistruth and denial of colossal proportions. It is now time for thinking peoples all over the Earth to step forward and own the true story about their ancestors, and where and how they lived.

There is much new information emerging that presents a more accurate picture of the ancient world. The civilizations in the Americas are far older than the current historical view presents. Knowing about the growth and development that occurred in earlier times will fill in the gaps and omissions that have been present for the past two thousand years. It has long been said that knowing who you are and from whence you have come will provide a base of understanding for the foundation of your life.

As people all over the Earth move into the coming age, certain negative thought forms need to be dispelled and removed from the human condition. One of the major ones is denial. It is important for all to see clearly the truth in any given situation. To perpetuate the idea that the Americas were lands only recently inhabited denies the numerous earlier cultures who lived and grew in the grace of the Almighty, leaving a rich and enduring heritage for those who were to come in the future.

The most significant record that has been left by these earlier peoples is their vibratory forcefield that beats with a deep and rich resonance. When one knows about them and attunes to them at a level of spirit, it will be possible to access a most important part of the human heritage that has been hidden for so long. We ask that those reading these words consider them seriously. Keep your mind open and inquiring as more new information comes forth about the earlier world. Access your inner knowing and intuitive sense about the accuracy of what emerges in the story of the human race on planet Earth. And participate with joy and enthusiasm in the process by which humankind is moving forward into wholeness.

## United States as Seed Carrier

The formation of the United States was an important step forward in the evolution of the Divine Plan. Many past cultures and civilizations served as stepping stones for the emergence of this key experiment in time and space. It was planned that a country dedicated to the principles of freedom and justice for all would emerge at a given time to offer itself as a cradle for the weary and downtrodden. There has been much pain on planet Earth as souls in incarnation have learned and experienced what it meant to be encased in matter by living within the various cultures that have been in ascendancy down through the ages.

The spiritual blueprint for this country has existed at the etheric level for all of eternity. But it was recognized that this country could only progress so far before its disintegration would have to set in. It is thus on the earthly plane in regard to every culture that surfaces for expression. But the high level of the ideals upon which the United States was founded and the intensity, with which it was developed in such a short time, predicated an early demise to the expression it carried.

This American culture was never intended to be long lived. Its purpose was to be a seed carrier for the development of future civilizations, which would embody varying principles upon which this country was founded. If it were to exist as a political entity over an extended period of time, a rigidity and crystallization would prevent the release and rebirth of these ideals in other designated areas of the Earth. It also is necessary that the evolutionary capsules be transmitted when the ideas are at their greatest strength. Only at this time is there a possibility for transference and success in establishing new cultures.

So do not be concerned about the disintegration and decay that you will observe in the years ahead. All is in divine order and right on schedule for the overall welfare of those on the planet. Truly, there is a new heaven and a new Earth being birthed on your planet, and many of the principles that were brought into being in the United States will serve as the foundation for the even greater cultures of the future.

There have been many civilizations in the past, which have placed a high value on the connection with the realm of spirit and the ensuing benefit found in bringing the information received to others. But the present American society emphasizes material and scientific matters above all else. This is not to negate the importance of the American archetypal experience in the evolutionary development of human beings on planet Earth. America, in its founding and its formation, has constituted a most significant step in the unfolding of the Divine Plan. It was here on this continent that the whole idea of individual rights and freedoms came into being in the current world age. To view oneself as a being with certain inalienable rights is an awareness that all souls must reach in their spiritual journey to reunion with The Creative Force. Until this knowledge becomes fully ingrained in the humus of soul knowing, one is truly functioning at a level of unconscious action.

So honor this great country of America. It has provided the stimulus for this evolutionary step forward. But in every great and significant experience lie the seeds of its dissolution and destruction. And so it is with America. The flip side of individual rights and responsibilities is individual license and self-centeredness. A true arrogance waits in the wings to surface when excess appears and dominates the purity of the ideal. You are living in a period when the negative side of this great concept is entering its dissolution phase. All that exists in God's world is of a cyclical nature. A pure Idea emerges for manifestation, develops into its finest expression and deteriorates into its negative aspect, so that it can end and provide the birthing ground for a new Idea to emerge for human experience and knowledge.

To understand this process is to honor the Tao or Way of Life. To own this process at a level of soul wisdom brings a sense of peace and harmony. One can recognize where one has been placed in the circle of life and how life will manifest. There is a peace that passes understanding and brings great harmony into the view one has of the life being lived. The people living in the East still recognize and practice the awareness of this concept. Now more and more individuals living in the West are coming to know and recognize the significance of this great spiritual truth. The cross-pollination of eastern ideas in the western world is preparing humankind for this giant evolutionary step forward which is about to be taken on planet Earth.

That is why there has been a proliferation of books and writings, as well as individual teachings, that have come into being to fertilize the awareness of receptive people all over the world. It is now time for disparate groups and beliefs to unite in celebration of the great beauty and power held within each soul existing in the many universes of time and space. There will soon be a great wave of subatomic particles wafting through creation, uplifting and transforming physical matter. All that exists in the many physical realms will be irradiated with the light of spirit, transforming the molecular nature of matter itself.

When this time comes, and it is on the horizon now, a new level of being will have arrived for everything that exists in the fields of matter. So constantly attune yourselves to the waves of spirit that are slowly infiltrating every crack and crevice of the many universes. For this is a comprehensive and all-encompassing event that has been sent out from the core of All That Is, and it is being felt at the most basic level throughout time and space. So honor this great spiritual event. Watch and recognize its unfolding qualities all about you. Let its essence permeate the many bodies that make up the reality of who you really are. Soon all receptive beings will find themselves in a dynamic process of cellular transformation not believed possible at the present time.

# A New Look at the Human Experience

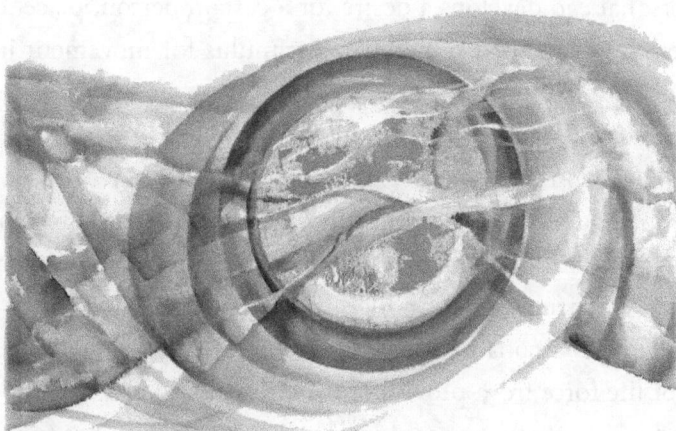

This period of time on the Earth is a most special one and will be remembered in the future as the pregnant pause before the Great Awakening occurred. Your world is on the brink of an evolutionary step forward, one it has been expecting for a long time. It takes many experiences to mold new consciousness. We have to repeat and repeat before true awareness sinks into the humus of the soul.

That is why one must never become discouraged when similar situations reappear in life. It can be likened to a dog gnawing on an old bone. It just takes a lot of gnawing in order to extract the meat from any learning experience. One of the primary activities of all beings is to grow in consciousness. It could be said that the universe is a vast school, which every soul is attending on a myriad of different levels.

# Desire and Fear

Think how different the approach to life would be if everyone embarked upon each life situation with the attitude that this was a lesson to be learned or an experience to enjoy. Most individuals act out of two modes — desire and fear. Desire is the motivating force behind much of the forward motion on the third dimensional level. Rarely is the highest good in any situation ever considered at the outset of an action. The personal ego develops a desire for a certain person, place, thing or experience, which then provides the stimulus for movement in a new direction.

Fear acts as a polar opposite to desire since its properties prevent or impede action. When fear exists on any level of the being, it immobilizes one and stops forward motion. A person in the throes of fear is virtually paralyzed and unable to perform what is required in any given situation. It is true that an individual can sometimes act when fearful, but fear causes a constriction of the etheric body, which prevents the prana or life force from providing the energy needed at the time.

And so it is that every soul in physical incarnation has to overcome these two hurdles to spiritualizing matter. For desire is the motivating force of the lower personality ego and rarely reflects the will of the higher self. Fear is a negation of the higher self, which never experiences this emotion at its level of being. The higher self is a center of love, wisdom and will. It is the ultimate purpose and goal of the higher self to be directly connected at all times to the personality ego, acting as an advisor during each physical incarnation.

The higher self is then connected to an even more advanced unit of spirit, which in turn is part of an ever-higher spiritual form. And so it goes. All is interconnected in the many universes of the Divine Creator. To know this is to be at peace at a profound level of being. This is what we are here to learn — that all of existence is One. When we truly know this ultimate truth at the innermost level of the soul, we will sink into the essence of the Godhead with a sweet cosmic sigh to sleep deeply until the next cycle of creation begins.

# Sin

We would like to speak to you regarding matters that pertain to current times on planet Earth. There is much that exists in the lives of human beings that must be reviewed and adjusted to reflect more accurately the truth of what really is. One concept, which has been preeminent in the belief system of humans for the past two thousand years, has been the concept of sin, and most particularly original sin.

The idea that humans are marked from birth with a basic flaw to living an uplifting and holy life is a totally erroneous idea. There really is no such thing as sin. It simply does not exist. There is no stain imprinted upon those that are birthed onto the Earth plane. On the contrary, all those who exist in the realms of matter have at their core an unsullied essence that is light and good with no impurities of any kind.

As human beings live on the Earth plane, they enter the realm of cause and effect and therefore are subject to the results of their choices and actions. When a child goes to school and makes mistakes or has difficulty learning a certain concept that eludes him or her, it is not said that the child is sinful. The child lacks knowing of what the right course of thought or action is. The child does not need someone to come and save him or her from the lack of knowing. On the contrary, the child just requires someone to continue assisting until a positive knowledge of what is true and good is reached. So the idea of Jesus the Christ coming to Earth to redeem those here for their evil ways and sins is a negative and inaccurate concept which is still widely held even today.

Life on the plane of matter is a learning experience. Those who perform hurtful or destructive acts are coming from a position of ignorance. They do not yet know that harming someone else is ultimately destructive towards themselves, since we are all one essence and inter-connected at a basic vibratory level. That is why the Law of Cause and Effect has been a great teaching tool. A person who harms another will experience the same pain until the knowledge and awareness develops regarding the error involved. Thus the individual learns at a primary level the inadvisability of negative, hurtful acts. Before that learning takes place, the person does not have the understanding necessary to make the choice that will uphold the highest good.

At no point in time is the individual sinful. The individual is just uneducated as to the ramifications of his or her actions. The concept of being flawed and marked with a great stain, as it were, is one of the greatest falsehoods perpetrated upon human beings on this planet. This idea originated from a religious hierarchy that has wanted to maintain ascendancy and control over its members, and for no other reason.

It is now time for earthlings to recognize the concept of sin for what it truly is. It is an attempt to keep those living on this planet from the knowledge that they are capable of maintaining an ongoing, primary connection with the Divine Source of All That Is. And that they have a part of themselves that is spirit — a perfect inner essence which is uplifting matter through an ongoing learning process, containing mistakes and errors in the unfolding. To see the purpose of human life as it truly is constitutes the most important awareness emerging at this time. Earth beings must know that they are part of a much larger picture, and that they play a key role in the spiritualizing of their universe.

This is why the idea of sin must be eradicated from the belief systems of those residing on the planet. Not only is the concept errone-ous, but it is severely limiting in all ways. Co-creating with the Divine Source, the birthright of all souls, is not possible when one sees oneself as being sinful. How can a sinful, flawed being create with an all-perfect Higher Source? When one believes that he or she is sinful, one cannot enter into the relationship that has always been available since the be-ginning of time. So we ask you who read these words to cast off this veil of ignorance and see the truth of who you are in the clear light of spirit. Then and only then will you be able to enter into a cooperative relationship with the Divine Creator of All That Is.

# Worry

Worry is the lower energy manifestation of vigilance and accurate scrutiny. When one worries, there occurs a close and ongoing observation of a certain person, place, thing or situation. To assess closely is a most important skill required of beings who occupy a field of higher density matter. In the earliest times on this planet, souls who incarnated in this forcefield had great difficulty sustaining a physical body. They were so attuned to spirit that they did not see or recognize the pitfalls of human existence and consequently lost the use of their physical vehicles because they did not observe the many obstacles and dangers that existed for them on this three-dimensional plane.

So a very necessary human characteristic was encoded in the genetic matrix of the human DNA. The ability to closely observe, assess, and analyze was moved into a more prominent position in the spectrum of human skills. As with anything that is positive and beneficial in this world of duality, there is a counter-balancing negative quality that also can manifest. To incorporate fully the wisdom of a human characteristic, one must experience all areas found within its essence. Then and only then does the mastery of that human behavior result in experiential wisdom, which becomes autonomic and no longer needs expression.

Throughout the many eons of human existence, the ability to be watchful and observe all elements of life going on around one has been honed and refined. But the fallout that has also occurred has been hypervigilance and worry over supposed or coming events. In the latter part of this Piscean Age with its Virgoan overlay, worry has been developed into an art form, particularly among women who have taken and owned it as if it were something precious and a sign of their caring.

Women have felt that to be truly effective they had to worry constant-ly about their children, their husbands, their homes, and their lives in general.

The negative pall that this human trait places on anyone that comes in contact with it is stultifying to the human spirit at all levels of exist-ence. It is now time in the upward evolution of humans on planet Earth to recognize that worry is the negative end of the spectrum that por-trays vigilance, scrutiny and keen awareness of all that occurs in one's environment. A truly conscious soul must always be attuned to what is occurring in its sphere of influence. This ability must be so ingrained that it becomes automatic and functioning all of the time.

We ask that you reflect upon these words at the deepest level of your being. The spiritualized human living on the Earth plane must have awareness honed to a basic skill. Then, as the irradiating pho-tonic particles continue to infiltrate their sphere in an ever-increasing intensity, humans will begin to expand their powers of observation into broader and ever greater realms and dimensions. Being encased in hu-man form is only one infinitesimal aspect of the entire soul entity that contains the human personality.

It is now time for humans living on the three-dimensional level of Earth to start to expand their consciousness into multidimensional awareness. In order to accomplish this step up on the spiral of life, the quality of worry has to be transmuted from its lower vibrational essence to the higher awareness of faith and trust in all that occurs.

Because underlying all aspects of consciousness, one must have the conviction at a deep level of knowing that the spiritual energy of the Godhead permeates every particle that exists, even down to the finest subatomic level. This energy is always unfolding what is for the highest good — even if it is not readily evident at the time. The ability to know and trust in the basic goodness of the Divinity is the underpinning of every realized being. This knowledge will sustain and uplift in times of darkness and great adversity and provide the peace that passes all understanding.

# Perfectionism

Emotionally, one of the biggest problems that a growing group of humans on the Earth plane is experiencing at this time is the wave of continuously surfacing human irritation. These feelings are accompanied with a mental clarity, which seems almost frightening. Many now see people, including themselves, in a way that exposes failings and weaknesses, which have always been there but never so evident. This capability is necessary in order to eradicate a great human failing — that of perfectionism. Only when we see with the clear eye of the eagle can we observe others and ourselves in the true light of spirit.

The first reaction to this type of sight is anger and disgust over the negativity viewed. Then the common response under these conditions is to try to correct the faults being observed. This course of action is particularly strong in anyone who has the character flaw of perfectionism. And lest you think you are one of few to experience this trait, you must know that almost all humans have some elements of this characteristic in their makeup. The reason this is so is because perfectionism is created out of pain and in no other way. And there are very few humans who have been able to heal and rise above their pain, whether it is physical, emotional, psychological or spiritual.

When an individual has experienced pain of any kind, the common reaction is always to do all in one's power to guarantee that the pain does not reappear under any circumstances. Once that commitment has been made, the human psyche is dedicated to a path of perfectionism, where effort is made to keep the cause of pain at bay no matter what the cost. An individual's world must be kept perfect in order to ward off the great hurt that pain brings. That is how this bane of perfectionism has grown to the predominance in human nature it now holds today. But it is understandable, is it not?

Perfectionism is a major drawback to the true health of an individual. This issue needs to be addressed by everyone who wants to progress on the spiritual path. The two cornerstones to the universes of the Creator are Truth and Love. It takes many existences to begin to discern the truth of any matter. Many experiences of trial and error have to occur before one can see with the clarity of spiritual truth. One of the final reactions, which has to be overcome, is that of one's negative response to viewing the imperfect. In the evolution of the soul, it takes a long time to learn to see clearly and without the obstruction of the human ego's personality. Also, societal pressures come into play, since striving for perfection is held as a very good thing in this day and age. And so it is that this issue has three distinctly different phases. The first phase is that of gaining the ability to see with clarity all that exists in one's life. The second is that of not reacting negatively to the less-than-perfect. And the third is the ability to love unconditionally the imperfect as a manifestation of the divine.

Quite a tall order, you might say! And truly it is a task of Herculean proportions, but not impossible. In fact, it is a test that must be passed in order for the soul to continue to progress up the spiral of life. And how does a person stay steady and not react adversely when faced with the faults of one's fellow beings, you might ask. It can only be done by assuming the role of the observer in every situation that arises in life. This stance becomes possible when one reaches the stage of development where it is known that he or she is a soul connected with its Source and operating out of a human body vehicle. Then and only then can one truly master the role of the observer.

When one observes, one watches the flow of life just as if seated by a river. The only difference is that what is being watched is the river of life. What must be learned here is that the observer never takes part in the action of the river's flow. You ask, "How can that be? To live in the world, I must be of it." Yes, this is true. That is why the human personality or ego was created, to carry the soul through each incarnation and serve as the vehicle for its manifestation in the world of matter. The personality engages in life in the world of matter, and the soul or higher self observes. Only when an individual's personality merges with the higher self can true and enduring wisdom is attained.

After one is firmly based in higher self-wisdom, then the task of experiencing love for all one sees, no matter how imperfect, is begun. This final act is of prime importance because the ultimate goal of Prime Creator is that all that exists be able to give divine love continuously. And so it now becomes evident why the conquering of perfectionism is such an important hurdle to be overcome on the soul's journey back to reunion with All That Is. Truth and Love are the twin pillars of divine creation. When all that exists

reflects them, the path of the soul has reached the completion of its journey. All is in Divine Order. All is One.

# Continuity

On rainy days, the water spirits refresh and renew the land with gentle moisture from the skies. As with other processes of nature on planet Earth at this time, rain is often viewed in a negative way. In the western world where outwardly directed movement is the norm, rain is seen as causing an interruption and cessation of activity. People feel disappointed when it rains and fail to recognize the great gift that is inherent in the nourishment of the land. In fact, all cultures rooted in a technological base have lost their connection to the natural processes of their world. They are no longer in attunement with the cycles and rhythms of the forces of nature. And they also have stopped interacting with these forces in a co-creative partnership, which their ancestors knew, honored, and followed.

The loss of the connection to the cycles of nature is only a symptom of a much greater loss — that of a deep knowing that all that exists is part of Prime Creator and that humans on Earth are an integral piece in the Divine Plan of All That Is. Because there is no longer an awareness of this fundamental truth, there is a corresponding loss in the knowledge held by humans that continuity or a continuous process is always at work in their lives. It provides a sense of purpose and security to know that one exists in an ongoing, dynamic continuum continually unfolding towards a positive and uplifting goal.

Continuity is provided by the coming and going of familial generations. To see parents, children, and grandchildren provides the awareness that there is a process creating one generation after another. To see, observe and participate in this process offers rightness and a sense of the drama of time ever unfolding in a beautiful luminous rhythm. Continuity provides hope and expectation, which uplifts the human spirit.

But continuity is much more than the march of generations ever onward. Continuity at its most basic essence is the foundation for the many universes themselves. For there exists always an undulating wave of spiritual mass known by many different names down through time. It is an all-pervading essence that wafts in an incredibly beautiful rhythm and continuous beat, never to be stopped except when periods of manifestation end. Then the beat becomes a pregnant stillness ready for activation upon the call of the One Primal Force.

To see continuity in this vein is to develop a firm trust in the ultimate goodness of all that transpires. No matter what is occurring at the outer level of life, to know that there is a steady, continuous divine rhythm of love and grace upholding all that is gives a great sense of peace, never to be lost, no matter what the circumstances are. Reflect on these words. True continuity exists at the fundamental base of all that is, both in spirit and matter. Let this knowledge sustain and uplift you always.

# Discrimination

There is a day, which is honored in your culture as the time of all souls, currently called Halloween. It is a period when powerful energy currents are abroad in the land. For many it is purely a day for play, masquerade, and revelry. But for those who function at a level of deeper consciousness or those who have experienced the dark side of this energy construct, this day carries with it a much different connotation. In earliest times in western culture, this day was called Hallowed Eve. The following day honored the great saints or higher beings who have guided and inspired the human race since its inception on this planet. And so it was that Hallowed Eve was set aside to prepare for this momentous time when an influx of high spiritual energies came into the planetary forcefield.

There are certain periods throughout each year when powerful vibrations of great magnitude are released from the higher dimensional levels to impulse the Earth as it moves forward on its evolutionary path. November 1st, as it is called currently, has long been recognized as one of those specially designated days. In earliest times, people withdrew from their ordinary activities on the day before, quieted themselves and raised their own personal vibration to be receptive to the energy emanations that would flood the Earth the following day. They lowered their lights and participated in whatever methods of prayer and meditation were used at the time. The evening was set aside as a time of attunement and going within. That is where the term Hallowed Eve originated.

Then when the following day dawned, people all over the Earth who followed these practices connected with the realm of the higher beings for guidance and inspiration in all areas of their lives. These beings were given many different names. In the western world, the term saint was the most widely used. In the eastern world, the designation of siddha or bodhisattva accurately described the high spiritual quality of these beings. For in those earlier times, the veil between the realms of spirit and matter was very thin, so there was direct knowing of their existence and much contact on a regular basis.

But, as in every area of life currently, the meaning of key times of the year has been distorted and totally reversed from its true essence. The holy evening of quiet prayer and attunement has become a time of noisy and boisterous revelry. Both adults and children dress in costume-like attire, which closely resembles the beings that reside in lower realms. Instead of preparing for the light, the humans in your culture honor and call forth the darkness. And then when the next day dawns, the reversal is again evident. Instead of a great day of spiritual significance that is honored by all, it is totally ignored. No rituals or celebrations occur whatsoever.

We are speaking to you about this topic to bring to the attention of all those who read these words the knowledge that human beings are dealing daily with the issue of great distortion in every area of their lives. The biblical phrase "seeing through a glass darkly" best expresses this phenomenon. It is important to recognize this fact. Much of what one sees about one is contrary to its true essence.

The American government's role is to serve its people. Instead it controls and manipulates the lives of its citizens. The stated purpose of the press is to inform objectively, and yet it distorts the news until the truth of what is being reported is shaded and lost. Americans profess a deep love for their land and yet allow it to be continuously polluted and despoiled for economic gain. Parents say they love their children, and yet they leave them for long periods of time in the care of others in order to increase their material wealth.

It seems as though the import of that of which we speak here is very negative indeed. But in truth it is not. For it is the prevailing reality that exists today. The native Americans in their religious beliefs honor the coyote as the expression of all that is contrary in life. They have known for ages that the reversal or opposite of truth is continuously being expressed in all areas of daily life. They describe the coyote as a great trickster in whom they find much amusement and fun. They were constantly on the watch for the trickster coming into their lives to reverse reality into a contrary state. They knew that this experience was part of the human condition. Therefore they never took themselves too seriously, because they knew that if they did the coyote would turn up and show them how foolishly they were acting.

The Native Americans' honoring of the function of the coyote in their society provided a leavening and a practical realism that kept them fairly in balance. They knew that trickery always was manifesting some-where and vigilantly examined every area of their lives for its expression. The current American culture operates from a naive acceptance of all that is presented as being true and accurate. Because of this belief, Americans are some of the most deluded people on the Earth.

The merging of the awareness of the newcomers to this land with that of their native-born predecessors will result in a widespread recognition that much deceit and trickery exists throughout American society. Then and only then will it be possible to effect the changes that need to occur in order for the United States to fulfill its purpose and charge within the Divine Plan.

So it is that one of the key skills that must be developed at this time is that of discrimination. Everything that comes before one must be viewed with the clear eye of the eagle. The truth and basic integrity of each situation must be discerned as accurately as possible. Where the contrary or opposite expression of the truth is manifesting, it must be recognized for what it is and laughingly rejected as an expression of the coyote trickster. For laughter and walking away from any person or situation is the most powerful way to eliminate its presence from one's life.

Believing distortions in truth or engaging in power struggles for supremacy only empowers the distortion more. So when one finds one-self in a situation where trickery exists, laugh as if at a great joke and walk away. There is nothing more deflating to deceit than laughter. Remember that the role of the trickster takes on cosmic proportions when seen in the mosaic of the unfolding of the Divine Plan. It forms the threshold into the holy of holies, which contains the two corner-stones of the universe — Truth and Love. Only when one understands and masters the role of the coyote can one see truth with a clear and knowing eye.

Prayer, meditation and visual imagery will help many of you to move out of those situations which are preventing you from proceeding on with your lives. But you will need to face the issue of how you see and deal with the negativity in your world in a more discriminating way. Many of you have entered and stayed in painful situations without any sense of the negative impact you were suffering to do so. When you develop knowledge and awareness of what you are doing, you will become much more self-protective.

You must recognize when you are being treated in a disrespectful or hurtful manner. The stance of many under these circumstances is to withdraw when this awareness arises. But this response comes out of victimization. That is not to say that there are not situations that warrant leaving, because there are. But when one leaves, it is with the strength and power of personal choice having been exercised after careful assessment of the conditions and the action needed to maintain balance.

And many times it will be necessary to remain within a negative dynamic for the service that can be rendered on a human level. When these occasions arise, careful discrimination will be required in order to provide the appropriate behavior for healing. So it would not be for the highest good to always respond by withdrawing from any given situation which has negative energy. But there is another important issue here to consider. And that involves the response one has after viewing the human flaws that exist in others. It is not necessary to help, correct or point out what you see. Only when you have reached the point where you can stand firmly and look at another with the eyes of love and understanding, no matter how distasteful his or her behavior, will you have mastered unconditional love.

## Love

We now would like to speak with you regarding the topic of love. Love is the most powerful force in the universe and upholds the very underpinning of all that is. The question asked so often is, "What really is love?" For very few experience this state as it was meant to be. Love is the essence of caring and connection for oneself, another or the God

Force. Its primary element is unity. Only when a feeling of union exists in any given situation or relationship can the vibratory essence said to be that of love.

What truly is union? It is a merging with someone or something other than one's self. This merging can manifest physically, emotionally, mentally or spiritually, either in whole or in part. When individuals come together to perform a sexual act, this is love occurring on the physical level. If an emotional connection also exists, the love vibration is stronger. If there is a meeting at the level of mind, the union of the two individuals is even more powerful. And if the beings can unite as souls, the love vibration has reached the highest level of union possible between two people.

And so we come to you to speak about this most important topic. The primary essence of the Creator is love that is accompanied by will, intelligence, and wisdom. The goal of creation is that all, which exists, become permeated with the divinity of love. Love can best be known and measured by the amount of light present at any given time. This is so because love is carried on the vibratory wavelength of light. The power of light magnifies the essence of love and spreads it into the farthest reaches of space, to be felt and absorbed by all of creation.

How does love manifest itself? This is a most important question indeed. We have said that love is caring, connection and union. We have also said that love is a vibratory wavelength found in every aspect of existence whether large or small. It is the very essence of creation and reflects the true nature of the Primary Force. Love is an energy that connects, nurtures, uplifts and sustains. It is found throughout the many universes of time and space.

Every human being living on planet Earth has encoded deep within the true nature of the Godhead. But many do not remember or recognize this truth. And so they feel a sense of incompletion and separation at the core of their being. The vibratory essence, which will bring wholeness at all levels, is love. As people learn to honor and care for themselves, they grow in love. As they learn to respect others, always acting from a place of integrity, they expand the power of love. We ask that human beings become more nurturing toward the planet and its many forms of life. Then love and light will infuse the Earth, bringing a radiance that moves out into the universe, transforming and uplifting all in its path.

Everything that exists on the many planes of spirit and matter is connected. Golden filaments of light interweave a web of power and beauty, touching all that lives. And so when the love vibration increases in force, the totality of existence experiences it in some manner. That is why even the smallest act of kindness has a far greater effect than can be imagined in this current age. When the science of energetics is more widely known, people will have a framework which will help them understand how thoughts and actions can impact at such a profound level.

And so we ask the readers of these words to reflect and meditate often upon the nature of love, doing all in their power to increase it in their lives. As you do this, you will become aware that love is expressed in a wide variety of ways. Sometimes love might appear to be uncaring. An example would be the parent who urges treatment and refuses to support the behavior of a child who is involved in drugs. It might appear to the child that the parent is acting in an unloving way. But the parent's love for the child mandates that the parent speaks in truth and withholds anything that would perpetuate the child's self-destructive behavior.

As the vibration of love grows and intensifies on the Earth, a totally new way of life will emerge, uplifting and transforming the current world from its pain and suffering. Distrust, greed, cruelty, and war cannot exist in a world in which the love vibration is paramount. And so the single most important thing anyone can do at this time is to focus on increasing love for self, for all those living on the Earth, and for the planet as well. Is it so much to care more, connect more and unite more at all levels? Try it. The impact of increased love in your life will change you forever. You will be reflecting your true birthright — one that has always been there for you, just a breath away.

# Death

We now would like to discuss with you the topic of death. In the earliest days of human habitation on the Earth plane, death was seen for what it really is — a time of transition containing both an ending and a beginning for the incarnating soul. It was recognized as an honorable process of completion to be faced with great joy and satisfaction no matter what the method of dying might be. If a person left the Earth plane in the early years or precipitously in a sudden death through accident or violent causes, the manner of the leave-taking was considered immaterial. The entire focus rested on honoring the completion of the life cycle and turning the attention to the joy of being back in the realm of spirit.

In those days, death was never viewed with fear or panic. It was part of the organic cycle of life, bringing to completion one more learning experience in the fields of matter. Grief or sorrow were never felt or expressed at the passing of a loved one. It was known at the deepest level of being that the same souls would meet again with new adventures to be experienced in different circumstances. Attention would then be turned to those still living. Interaction with the departed one would happen only when and if the necessity arose. The veil between the many realms of spirit is very thin indeed. Other dimensions overlap and fold into matter in a continuous undulating fashion. Any contact that is needed is only a heartbeat away, figuratively speaking.

In the western world, death is a process charged with fear, denial and loathing. Many refuse to even acknowledge it and exist as if life were a gift from the gods of unending immortality. They seem to have no recognition of the consequences of their actions in regard to the maintenance of their physical bodies. Others hold the idea of death close to them and gnaw on it like an old friendly bone. All their planning and expectations center around the preparation for death. At an early time, they start to think of death as imminent and expect it in a very real way.

Seldom in these times is there a knowledgeable and realistic view of death, as this transitional phase is called. Death is part and parcel of the ongoing process of life. It is a transmutative step in the continuous cycle of creation. Many times in the past, physical bodies were imbued with great life force, which allowed them to exist in form for long periods. But the electromagnetic forcefield of the planet now carries a weaker frequency, which reduces the longevity of humans living on the Earth plane. But no matter the length of the life, at some point in time it ends so that a new cycle of manifestation can begin with fresh experiences that will enhance the growth of the soul.

Never has it been possible to live in form without any change. All that exists in the fields of matter is subject to the Law of Change. So humans fall into the same pattern that all of life does throughout the universes of the Creator. It was always so, down through the many eons of time and space. But cessation of consciousness viewed as the ultimate end of life never occurs in the world of spirit/matter. Energy just transmutes to another form or essence that continues to contain the consciousness of the former body/mind continuum.

So all that has existed since the beginning still exists. It can never end or be destroyed. Of course, the physical sheath that holds the unit of consciousness can change its role as the carrier of the soul essence. But the mind force still exists to create new vehicles for expression and learning. Therefore when a person dies, it is important to know that one can access the consciousness of that being through strong intent and openness. Usually the issue of respect for the dead person's journey prevents one from doing so, and dependency is never encouraged in any form. It is important to note, however, that contact can be established with one who is residing on the spirit plane if it is for the highest good of both of the souls involved.

The totality of what has occurred since the beginning of time and what will exist in the future is contained in an egglike mass of waves and particles penetrating and interacting like a percolating stew, of divine proportions. In the coming age, it will be known by all that death is a positive part of the human condition. The veil separating the worlds of matter and spirit will be nonexistent. Grief and loss expressed over the death of loved ones will no longer be the norm. Interaction of beings on various dimensional levels will be commonplace and will occur for many reasons with great regularity. The unfolding world of the future will be a wondrous place indeed!

# Relationships

We would now like to talk with you about interpersonal relationships, which form the basis for all contact between human beings. Except for the destructive forces of nature impacting the lives of those residing on the Earth plane, most of the pain and suffering that is experienced arises from the hurtful actions of one against another. For you see, a major aspect of the Divine Plan is to provide a crucible where the growth and development of the soul can occur. That crucible is human interaction within the framework of interpersonal relationships.

If one were to look closely at all the phases of one's life, it would be immediately evident where the greatest pain and suffering lies. Think of the continuous struggles that are in evidence between individuals, groups and nations all over the planet. The human personality constantly attempts to gain supremacy for itself in any type of situation with another.

The need for approval, personal gratification and ego satisfaction is most often the paramount factor operating when human interaction occurs. When these needs are not met for whatever reason, negative and hurtful responses are forthcoming. Then personal power struggles commence, causing physical, emotional and psychological pain, which is the lot of all souls incarnating on Earth.

It is now time for those who are the pioneers of a new age and species to face this issue in an honest and forthright fashion. Negative human interaction based on the factors just mentioned has to be eradicated from the human condition. It is no longer acceptable in any form. For, you see, all of those living within the many universes of time and space are moving towards total attunement with their Creator, whose primary essence is love.

Hurtful actions towards oneself or others cannot exist within the construct of love. These two states are incompatible in all ways. It is part of the Divine Plan at this point in time to bring the issue of interpersonal relationships into focus in order that they can rise to a higher level of functioning for all beings.

## Reconciling Differences

Very few relationships have any longevity at this time, because they are constituted on false and inaccurate assumptions. No longer are the old ways of relating able to continue. In this current period, people will have to come to terms with what constitutes a healthy relationship in order for it to endure.

So as you look at your own life and those whom you know about you, you will see this theme surfacing on an ever more intense level. Soon it will be known that, in order for a relationship to be successful, certain qualities will need to exist. And this applies not only to individuals but to groups also. First and foremost, people must come together in love and respect. By love we mean the impersonal type of love known as "agape" to the ancient Greeks — the love for one's fellow beings as members of the human race.

Respect and honoring of one another is essential in developing an ongoing relationship. This respect will be shown by allowing other people to be who they are without changing them in any way. The biggest problem in interpersonal relationships in this day and age can be found in the area of reconciling differences. It seems to be increasingly difficult for individuals, groups, or nations to be able to accept and honor the differences that exist between them. In many cases, a struggle for supremacy of one's own way is seen as the most effective method of solving the disharmony.

But in reality, this method is the least successful of all. The spiritual law governing respect says that everything is existence must be recognized and honored for what it is, no matter how negative or distasteful, because that is its current state. For one to try to change another person is intrusive and disrespectful. So one might ask, "How can the actions that need improvement in people and situations be addressed?"

The answer is quite simple. Every human being needs to strive for the highest level of behavior for oneself and then towards others. Accompanying this commitment is the recognition that no expectations can be held in regard to the behavior of others. How they act is their own responsibility. But we do not wish to imply here that the behavior of others

should be endured if one is impacted adversely. To do so would be a spiritual failing of major proportions.

What we are asking the readers of these words to consider is accepting the reality of all situations. If a person acts in a certain way, accept that action as an expression of how the person feels at that time. Do not react if it is displeasing. Just watch what transpires in a detached manner. Accept the action for what it is and currently represents, nothing more. Do not respond with any attempt to change or modify the other's behavior in any way. If it is not pleasing to you, remove yourself in a graceful manner from any further interaction at the time.

You may ask, "How can individual differences be reconciled to reflect harmony in human relationships?" If you can intuit this great truth, you will have learned one of the secrets of the universe. For, you see, this question is at the core of each and every relationship, which exists throughout time and space. There are no two soul essences that are identical anywhere. In this universe, which has duality as its primary theme, most enduring relationships have to deal with the issue of innate differences manifesting continuously. The great challenge is to discover how these differences can interact always with love and respect and not disharmony. In any relationship where there is considerable similarity, stasis and stagnation become the foundation for the interaction. There is not enough diversity to provide the humus for increased growth and development.

The common refrain in partnerships is "Oh, how I wish my partner were more like I am!" If that desire could be seen carried through to fulfillment, it would be evident in a moment how stifling that would be. So honor the variety of human expression all about you. Know that all of interpersonal interaction is merely the play of the Divine Creator experiencing in the fields of matter. Release the dramas and power struggles. They are a complete waste of time, consuming an untold amount of energy that is meant to be directed into creative self-expression.

Remember what you came here for. All beings are playing a cosmic game of hide-and-seek. We are all here to find the treasure at the end of the rainbow. We are sparks of spirit created by the Source of All That Is. We came to play throughout the many universes of time and space, developing more light and brilliance until we ultimately discover who we really are and return to our true home. It is so simple, is it not? Think on these words. Do the lives you are living now reflect this great truth? If not, start to incorporate the knowledge of spirit in all that you do. You will find that you will be lifted onto a higher turn of the spiral to grow far beyond what you can ever imagine.

The single most significant issue to be learned now on planet Earth is that no person needs to be with anyone in any situation which is counter to their soul's best interest. One can simply decline and seek a better personal course. When people in any type of relationship cannot agree on a given action, then each person must follow what seems best, even if it is different. Following this approach will bring a harmony and balance into the relationships with others far beyond what these simple words seem to imply. Think of the freedom and release from tension that this concept holds.

No longer does one have to do what others want and expect unless it is in harmony with one's higher self. And if all actions are in harmony with one's soul wisdom, then truly they will be for the highest good. So the most important ability to be developed in all areas of life, but particularly interpersonal relationships, will be the accessing of one's inner knowing. This is meant to be the guiding force in the lives of those living on the Earth plane. The inner self-wisdom is all loving and knows what is for the highest good in any situation. It can best be reached when one is in a state of prayerful receptivity or meditation.

This is why we emphasize continually the importance of regular, silent attunement to the realm of spirit as the basic foundation for one's life. When one follows this practice, the ability to know the right course of action or inaction with self or others is readily available for any situation in life. When true love and respect become the norm in human relationships, there will be the dawning of a new heaven and a new Earth long predicted down through the ages.

## Relationships and the Physical Environment

Interpersonal relationships are extremely significant and play a key role in the spiritual journey unfolding at this time. In earlier ages, different issues and experiences provided the setting for expansion of the human spirit. The ability to work in harmony with nature on all levels was a primary emphasis for Earth beings. Then came the time of the emergence of great civilizations. These cultures learned about living and prospering within fixed societal structures that imposed limitations and demands upon the individual will. At the same time, individuals in incarnation had to struggle with their relationship to a higher spiritual power which required so much from them — at times even their lives in sacrifice.

So humans on this planet have traveled a long road to reach this point where the arena for soul growth now resides in the interpersonal relationships with parent, child, partner, friend and fellow worker. In these settings, there is much to learn about one's own capacity to interact with others in a loving and positive way. What is becoming evident is that in order for one to relate at an optimum level with another, ongoing inner personal work must occur.

If one feels anger, resentment, grief or fear within his or her essence, it will be projected out on to the outer world and those nearest in it. Everything we experience is merely a reflection of our inner state of mind and emotion. As our mental state evolves and changes, our outer circumstances also shift to form a compatible alignment.

The awareness is just emerging into human consciousness that we truly do create our own reality in a far more direct way than we have known. So great progress is occurring all over the planet as human beings awaken and realize that they are truly the creators of their own destiny. Many recognize this knowing deep within and allow themselves to be transformed at a profound level of being.

As these inner changes occur, much negative vibratory energy is being released into the atmospheric shield surrounding the Earth. This release is also contributing to the worsening of the climate and impacting the Earth's crust, causing more earthquakes and volcanic activity. In the future, there will be an expanded awareness concerning the impact that our thoughts, words and actions have on the physical well being of the planet and its climatic and atmospheric conditions.

The entire system of life will be recognized as interdependent at a basic molecular level. All animate and inanimate life is interactive and connected. A negative or hurtful situation will cause an effect far more extensive than is recognized at this time. For this reason, each individual living within the three-dimensional realm must take personal responsibility for his or her impact upon life as it unfolds in their area. Political dissention and turmoil can result in extensive rain and flooding to a most unusual degree. These weather conditions are merely the automatic atmospheric response to negative human activity. Intense anger and upset creates the need for cooling rains to tone down and dampen the angry rhetoric that has polluted the air itself.

What is most important to note here is that everything a human being thinks, says or does has an immediate impact on others and the actual physical environment. Also, Prime Creator has built into every system in the universe a self-regulating corrective mechanism that restores harmony and balance. It is truly beautiful, is it not? Reflect on these words.

Start to take responsibility for all that you do. Learn to transmute negativity into positive creative energy. Interact with the forces of nature. Far more than you realize, they are reflecting the state of the beings within their environs. Learn to create optimal weather conditions not only in your physical environment but in your human relationships as well.

## Attaining Positive Relationships

Human interaction is generally bumpy at best and cannot be given the significance that many apply to it in this day and age. By this we mean that the amount of emphasis placed in this current age on the importance of relationships is out of balance with the other major areas of life. When human beings grow to understand each other at a soul level, there will be a deeper awareness about what constitutes positive relationships in every type of situation. Then, and only then, can the intensity of forming successful relationships assume lesser importance.

Currently, a common human response to problematic relationships is to walk away from situations and people when they are distressing. Sometimes this is the wisest course of action. But in other circumstances, it is necessary to remain and participate in the play of consciousness that is unfolding. When one does stay in an uncomfortable situation, for whatever reason, it is really important to be centered and empowered. The most effective stance in this type of matter is for one to be detached enough to flow with the energy of the moment in a positive way.

The energetics of interpersonal give and take are at the base of every human interaction. Everything that exists in the many worlds of the Creator is basic energy in varying forms. As souls on every plane grow to see the energy all about them, they will know instantly what type of intention exists in the statements and actions of others.

The practice that currently exists on the Earth plane of attacking others verbally with the appearance of joking or humor will be seen for what it really is — an attempt to demean someone using the mask of humor to disguise the true intent. As human society has moved away from warfare and hand-to-hand combat as the accepted way of settling disputes, aggression has been masked behind verbal affronts, some of which are presented in a joking mode. The perpetrator of this action is attempting to hide negative feelings behind a facade of supposed humor.

One of the most important developments at the present time is the outstanding work that is being done by some in the area of personal thoughts and emotions. More and more people are interested in clearing their emotional bodies of the residue of negativity that exists within them. They are taking responsibility for the impact their thoughts and actions have on others. Also, they are recognizing when others are directing negativity and ill will toward them, even though it is couched in the apparently acceptable behavior of joking or teasing.

This ability to read accurately the intent behind others' actions, no matter what the presentation, will become the norm for interpersonal relationships in the future. When people can feel and see the true energy of every situation, human beings' behavior towards each other will change for the better. Every human contact will be seen for what it really is, by those involved and by those who are only spectators. It will be impossible to hide what is really being thought and felt at any given point in time.

This current age is experiencing the most difficult period in this process of attaining true and positive relationships. For only a small number of people have done the important work of emotional healing. An even smaller number is aware that energy in its varying forms constitutes the base for every action and reaction between individuals and groups. Even those who recognize this fact are still unable to put what they know into effect in a practical manner.

Think about what we have said here for a moment. The base of all that exists in the many worlds of spirit and matter is energy. Energy coalesces and solidifies to create matter. Matter takes on the appearance of solid structure, but is still energy in its basic form. Every interaction between two human beings is an interplay of energy forces. So to really understand the true essence of what is happening, it is necessary to see and assess what type of energy is being transmitted from one person to another. The ability to do this is emerging in humans all over the Earth at the present time.

Secrets, falsehoods, and deceit will become a thing of the past, because what is being felt and thought will be recognized in every person's electromagnetic forcefield. At this time, classes are springing up in various locales that teach people how to see and read auras. There are books in print showing what various thoughts look like in color and form. Anger, hate and envy will be seen for what they really are and will not be hidden behind an apparently jovial or laughing manner.

In this period when these capabilities are just starting to emerge, the most important quality that a person can have is that of personal integrity. One must take responsibility for one's own negativity, declare it unacceptable and eradicate it from the personality matrix. One must also refuse to be the object of another's negativity and also must not return in kind what one has received. We know that what we are asking is difficult, but it must be accomplished for personal freedom to be gained. If one is pulled into another's negativity, one gives power and recognition to that state.

An individual must reject and repel any type of energy that feels bad or uncomfortable. This can be done in a wide variety of ways. One can quietly remove oneself from the situation without bringing attention to what is transpiring. One can also speak to what is being seen and felt in a way which does not demean or detract.

A most effective way to deal with this situation is to rise above the human interaction and relate directly with the other's higher self. Express love and regret at what is happening and request a change of attitude and behavior. If the individual displaying the negativity is so shut off from his or her higher wisdom, then at least love has been expressed and no other responsibility for involvement is necessary. One can remove oneself personally from any more interactions.

In some cases, particularly when family is involved, it may be considered undesirable to leave for a number of reasons. If the individual decides to stay in a situation where negativity is continually being expressed, then a mode of personal protection must be devised with an accompanying detachment and empowerment in effect at all times. One must never allow oneself to engage in retaliation of any kind. If this cannot be guaranteed, then it will be necessary to leave in order to keep the integrity of one's soul essence intact.

So we ask that all those who read these words reflect upon them at length and apply them to any situation existing in your life. You are all at the point in time where interpersonal relationships must reach a higher level of interaction. It is one of the most important advancements that must occur in order for the human race to move to a better level of functioning. The great harm done by individuals, groups and nations to each other must come to an end. Those who can rise above the old ways and act in a more loving manner to all will truly be the progenitors of the newly emerging species which will inhabit the Earth in the era to come.

## Relationships in the Future

One of the most difficult experiences for Earth beings to master is interpersonal interaction. The reason for this is very complex indeed. All that comprises an individual's personal makeup comes into play whenever one enters into a situation in which relating to another is involved. For, you see, each being is totally unique, a compilation of all the many experiences which molded and formed that soul down through the eons of existence. Just think of this concept for a moment. Visualize the journey of any given soul. Try to see in your mind's eye a single being moving from one incarnation to another, gathering knowledge through the many different lifetimes, which develop the soul into an individualized unit of spirit.

The peace and wisdom is gained from living in the many fields of the Divine Creator and learning what the very existence of life in all its many forms is about. This is the underlying purpose for all of existence — simply to be. Many different realms have been created to serve as stages for the growth of knowledge and wisdom. These realms all exist as energy matrices for the development of the soul, both in individual and group form. For the primary level of experience is the individual soul unit. The next step in development is the merging of the soul with a larger group soul entity for the purposes of expansion and further learning in a different setting.

So one can see that the variables for each soul's growth are infinite. And with each new living situation, awareness is gained that adds another facet to the diamond, which is the soul of the individual. Some experiences are beautiful and uplifting, providing a glimpse of the divine perfection, waiting at the end of the journey. Others are painful and difficult, serving more as the grit that produces the lustrous pearl through ongoing friction. But the ultimate outcome for all of these sparks of spirit is that they develop a truly unique awareness of what it is to exist in the universes of the Divine Creator.

Therefore it is easier to understand the complexities involved when one or more beings come together in the arena of interpersonal interaction. Each prior learning of the soul creates an element within the persona that is expressed in the ensuing thoughts, words and actions with others. For we are all simply a composite of our previous experiences in the many realms of time and space. Based on what we have learned, we act in certain ways which reflect that learning. If the coming together of two beings could be seen in a kaleidoscope of color, each thought, word or action would take on a different hue based on the individual's frame of reference.

It will become readily apparent how delicate and sensitive every human exchange truly is. Each thought, even unexpressed, registers at a certain level and is picked up by those who are in the vicinity of the individual. They, in turn, react based upon their own frame of reference. This is just a small indication of the depth and complexity that is part and parcel of every interpersonal contact.

Humans in the future will have the ability to see the electromagnetic forcefield of others about them. Being able to do this will open up an entire level of understanding about the experience and basic makeup of all with whom one comes in contact. Think of this concept for a moment. It will be possible to see in the auras surrounding other bodies the distillation of all the experiences which have molded and formed that being. The strengths and weaknesses will be readily apparent in colors emanating from the inner self. So at an immediate glance it will be apparent who a person is and what he or she has learned down through the eons of time.

In the coming era, deception will become impossible at all levels. Deceit will be seen clearly in the auric forcefield surrounding the body. Others with whom an untruthful person is interacting will speak immediately to what they are observing in the individual's energy field, causing a correction to occur. Will this not be truly wondrous indeed?

Think of all the pain that is currently caused by untrue thoughts, words and deeds. This pain will be eradicated by the addition of the human ability to see the energy field of others. Those living on the

Earth plane are starting in a few instances to develop this capability. At this point in time, seeing auras is a skill that must be learned through the raising of consciousness and practice in developing second sight. But after enough people have acquired this capability, reading energy fields will become a part of the autonomic nervous system and will be performed by all.

You ask, "How can this ability be developed by those living at the current time?" It truly is very simple. One must raise the vibrational level of the body to perform this higher function. This is accomplished by attuning to higher dimensional vibrations through meditation and contemplation. By quieting oneself and going within to the center of inner stillness, it is possible to activate the mechanism that expands the ability to see at the third-dimensional level. Then the next step is to look at a person or object with the knowing and expectation that you can see the colors and forms found within the electromagnetic field. Reflect on these words and try what we suggest. It will bring a true awakening indeed.

Once humans will have grown in capability to the point where they can see the auras of those about them, it will be possible to view in an instant what the composite experience of each soul has been. The aura surrounding each one will contain a distillation of all that has happened to that soul.

It will also be possible to see how the person is reacting to each and every word and thought. Think of this concept. What a different world it will be when everyone is recognized for who they are and what they are thinking and doing at any given moment. There will be instant accountability for all. What a wondrous place planet Earth will be when people take another great step forward towards living in the light of truth and love — the final state for which we all were created.

# Sexuality

We now would like to speak about human sexuality, one of the most significant areas of life for each incarnating soul. For you see, sexuality and all the ramifications of this experience play a key role in the development of each soul who resides on the Earth. When spiritual beings first came to this planet, they were androgynous and possessed the essences of both male and female within themselves. They could reproduce through mental thought and therefore did not require a partner of the opposite sex. But as these souls began to solidify into ever more dense forms, it became difficult to bring forth other humans in this manner.

And so it was that a new phase in human evolution came into being. The polarity of male and female in human form was created. With it came the need for a man and woman to join together in sexual union in order to produce offspring. As males and females played and experimented with this powerful dynamic, human sexuality became a major factor in the lives of everyone living on planet Earth. This was so because of the power of sexual union and its impact on the bodies and emotions of those experiencing it. The Creative Forces responsible for bringing human sexuality into manifestation imbued the act with tremendous attraction so that the reproduction of the human species could be guaranteed.

The primary reason the act of sexual intercourse is so significant for men and women on Earth is because of the qualities of human response that are felt during the act. All souls living on the Earth plane feel a sense of separation from the Source of All That Is. It is particularly so at the present time. The experience of the sexual act contains within it intense joy and union that mirrors in a lesser manner what the soul feels when joined to the spiritual essence of the universe. The sensations of union experienced in the sexual act are deeply needed by souls who have forgotten their own spiritual connection to the Creative Force.

And so it is that individuals come together sexually seeking something much deeper than they really understand at a conscious level. And also there are forces generated during these acts that have an impact far beyond what is realized by those involved. Sexual union carries within itself a vortex of powerful energies that are released into the forcefield of those participating and remains there for some time. In ancient times, people knew this and therefore were careful and selective about those with whom they joined in such an important and intimate act.

In those early times, men and women came together with a deep commitment to share love and joy with each other in a way that mirrored spiritual union with the Creator. There was expressed a gentle and caring respect by the participants as they honored and loved each other. If the sexual union was for the purpose of procreation, then both the potential father and mother made specific preparations. They purified, cleansed and raised their vibratory rate to the highest levels possible in order to offer the incoming soul a hospitable environment in which to incarnate.

But as the Divine Spiral turned and human beings sunk deeper into matter, the knowledge concerning the spiritual significance of human sexuality slowly eroded and was lost. This has been so particularly in the past four thousand years, when the worship of the Divine Feminine has been subverted and repressed in cultures all over the Earth. As the male principle became dominant on the planet, the honor and respect for women diminished. Sexuality developed into acts initiated and controlled by men. Women were viewed as subjects or vassals to be used as men saw fit. The needs and desires of women were immaterial and ignored much of the time.

As the past four thousand years have unfolded, male dominance affected the human sexual act in countless ways that undermined its divine purpose. As warring armies conquered new lands, rape and pillage of women and children were accepted practice. Even in the Americas, different tribes raided their neighbors for women and children who would serve as slaves to be used as they saw fit.

The long-established concepts of love and respect for the feminine principle in all of life were ignored and defiled. Rape became an accepted action used by men to dominate and use women as they pleased. The time-honored sexual practices of mutual honor and consent became a thing of the past in most relationships. Even until recent years in the United States of America, one of the most progressive of nations on the Earth, women and children were considered the property of a male and had no individual rights within the law.

Under these conditions, human sexuality lost its sacredness and deteriorated into burdensome compliance for many women. This is not to say that relationships did not exist where mutual love and honor were present. But they were very rare indeed. And forced sex within the confines of societal mores extended to children as well as women. Incest has been a common and long-held practice for literally thousands of years. It is true that many cultures have laws and taboos forbidding this act of shared sexual intimacy within families. But what has been actually happening in the privacy of the home has been very different.

We must take some time here to speak to the harm and impact that incest has for the individuals involved, as well as for the very fabric of the family and society at large. Developing sexuality within each and every human being has a divine rhythm that unfolds in a pattern most appropriate for the individual's physical and emotional growth and development. When sexual activity is initiated too early, the rhythm of a human's unfolding sexual cycle is interrupted. Coping with the powerful forces of human sexuality is introduced before one is ready for the impact. And we are not just speaking of sexual activity within the family group. We also are referring to any sexual act performed before the right age and time.

There has always been a rhythm in the affairs of humans living on the Earth plane. The knowledge of and attunement to these rhythms has slowly eroded and been lost over the centuries. Many rituals used to exist all over the planet recognizing and honoring the passages made by each individual throughout life. These rituals came into existence to bring awareness to the significance of key periods and events. They allowed people to reflect upon where they were in life and to see the importance of what they were experiencing in societal as well as personal terms.

These rituals and practices grew out of a clear recognition of each phase of human development and how it related directly to the evolutionary process. Many cultures realized the importance of the rhythms and patterns in life being experienced at the right time in order for true harmony to exist. This recognition has broken down and has been lost, causing an imbalance of major proportions at the level of societies all over the Earth. This truth is known, although possibly not consciously, by everyone in incarnation on the Earth plane today.

And so it is that one area of healing that is emerging at this time is a return to the honoring and recognition of the rhythms and cycles of the Earth and the humans who live upon it. In the coming age, which all are presently entering, the reestablishing of harmony and balance will become the order of the day. This will be especially so in the next two to three hundred years. Those living on Earth will look back to these times we have been discussing and see them as an unfortunate period of dark and painful events through which humanity lived in order to rise into the light of spirit.

## Human Sexuality in the Future

We would like to focus on where humans are now in regard to this issue of sexuality and what will be unfolding for them in the future. For some time, human sexuality with all of its attending practices has been going through a shift of major proportions, particularly in the western world. As the reemergence of the feminine principle has increased in power and intensity, it has had a major impact between men and women in the area of sexuality. Women have started to honor their sexuality and increasingly have refused to abide by the deeply entrenched mores of society.

Women also have taken the initiative in defining who they are and just what they are willing to do in regard to sexual relations with men. No longer will they be docile and passive recipients of men's desires and wishes. They are choosing their partners in a more assertive way and are rejecting any partners that are not pleasing to them. But as women become more sexually active with men of their own choice, they are falling into negative patterns of behavior, just as men did earlier.

In order to proclaim their freedom from old restrictions and limitations, they have become driven by desire and have fallen into license. In so doing they have repeated male patterns of willful irresponsibility, not only to themselves but also to their partners. They have forgotten the values of purity, integrity and honor that have always been implicit in the feminine psyche. The great creative forces of the universe gave men the role of impregnator of the divine seed in a way that mirrored the strength and power of spirit. To women these great forces gave fecundity and receptivity, which served as a sacred vessel where the love of the couple was transmuted into a radiant expression of human divinity.

We do not want to give the impression that this act of love is not meant to be fun and playful on a human level. For that is truly an important element within sexual coupling. For all of those who will read these words, we are attempting to reawaken your deeply held knowledge regarding the divine pattern that was imprinted upon you in regard to the meaning of sexuality. And therefore we will summarize for you in rather succinct statements the prime concepts that were encoded in human sexuality at the outset of its creation.

Sexual union between a man and a woman is a reflection in a lesser way of the attunement of the soul to the Divine Creator. It is an act to be entered into with great love and respect by both participants. It is never to be done for the primary purpose of physical gratification alone. It is to be recognized as a sacred ritual releasing powerful vibratory energies. These energies intermingle with the couple making love and move out into the very cosmos itself in a radiance of unbelievable beauty.

Men and women need to be conscious of all that sexuality entails. They need to choose their partners in a discriminating way. Love and honor for the other need to be felt always by both partners. No act of physical union should occur if these two feelings are not present. This means that force can never be a part of the sexual act between two people. Also the timing of each individual's personal sexual unfolding must always be respected. Never is the sexual act to be performed by one who is not ready for the intense vibrations released into his or her energy field.

Children are to be conceived with intent. Physical, emotional, psychological and spiritual preparation needs to be made by a man and woman who are to serve as the vehicles for an incarnating soul. All of life is to be honored and protected as an expression of the Prime Creator. No child is to be conceived without the commitment to love and nurture being present. This needs to be true not only for the parents but also for all of the society within which the child will be born.

The intent of the sexual act was that it be performed between loving, consenting adults. In the coming age, the feelings of love and honor will be recognized as the primary motivator between two individuals. The sexual orientation of the two will be left solely to the participants, with no judgements made by society as to morality or acceptability. It will become widely accepted that respect and love for each other are what need to be present when consenting adults come together in an act of sexual union.

## Infidelity and Commitment

One of the areas of greatest suffering between men and women down through the ages has been sexual infidelity. There are two polarities working against each other in this issue, creating a crucible for transformation within those incarnating on the Earth plane. The polarities are unfaithfulness and commitment. When two individuals come together and enter into the intimacy of sexual union, a bond of powerful force is created which is not recognized in this day and age.

The current era of open and free sexuality has come as a reaction to the strict mores of the earlier Puritan and Victorian societies of England that set the tone for western society in recent centuries. In order for balance to be reestablished, there needed to be a period for the antithesis of these sexually repressive eras to hold sway in the affairs of humans. But during these current times of rampant sexuality, the earlier knowledge regarding the impact and effect of coming together in sexual union has been lost.

Only now, with the scare of sexually transmitted diseases in evidence all over the globe, is a faint glimmer of awareness beginning to dawn. People are beginning to recognize that performing a sexual act with someone connects them in a sense with all earlier partners with whom that person has joined. Even though possible infection is the impetus for this emerging recognition, it is touching very faintly on some of the energy dynamics found in the sexual act.

There is no more intimate act between humans on the Earth plane at this time than sexual union. Not only do the two people coming together sexually merge their bodies, but also at a deeper level they merge their multilayered energy fields in a co-mingling imprint that stays with them for some time. This influence has a more profound effect than can be comprehended. This is why a careful and discriminating selection needs to be made before entering into a sexual act. Impulsive and brief couplings of people for closeness or sexual gratification have an effect upon them at many levels of body, mind and spirit.

So when two people come together in a relationship of any sort, an even greater dynamic comes into play. Once they express their love, perform an act of sexual union, and make a commitment to each other, a merger occurs that is registered on many different levels of both spirit and matter. Also, a spiritual construct is created that exists outside of the energy fields of the partners, which is a synthesis of who they are and what they can become together.

This is why there is such deep suffering when one of the individuals in a relationship is unfaithful by joining with another or wants to end the relationship. It is not possible to end a love affair with someone without a painful period of disengagement. Even if one is emotionally disconnected or has found a new partner, the dismantling of the energy fields has to take place. This process can be said to mirror death in many ways, since in reality the relationship is dying on a variety of levels.

Dealing with the polar opposites of human commitment and infidelity is one of the most significant hurdles humans have to face in spiritual growth and development. When one is committed, there is a pledge given which is not broken unless the partners come to the recognition that the end of the relationship is in the best interests of both concerned. Then time needs to be given to a caring and sensitive dismantling of the energy of the relationship on all levels.

And so it is that humans have come together down through the ages to join, commit, and then struggle with unfaithfulness. Many lifetimes are lived in which a soul experiences all sides of this issue. In one existence, a person can play the role of the unfaithful partner. In another lifetime, that person can be the one wronged. On and on the spiral unfolds. But once the recognition is gained as to what it means to be faithful and the will to do so is created in the face of all that is tempting, infidelity no longer becomes an issue for that soul. Then the soul is able to embark upon a relationship and remain constant always.

However, we would like to take a moment to speak to the subject of honor and respect, the cornerstone of any relationship. If they do not exist in a partnership, or if an element of abuse is present in any form, then commitment in those circumstances would be destructive to the soul and should never be given. This distinction is crucial in this day and age when abuse of all kinds is so prevalent in relationships.

And so it is that we ask all who read these words to think about what has been said here. It is now time for infidelity to be addressed by the humans on planet Earth. This is why this issue has been reflected in the actions of many prominent people in public life. They are serving as catalysts and mirrors in order that all of you can come to terms with this painful human failing and eradicate it from the arena of interpersonal relationships. Once this is so, life on Earth will step up to a higher spiritual level. When human beings can come together to love and uplift each other by always being caring of each other's souls, there truly will be a new heaven and a new Earth on this planet.

# Addictions

There is a topic that must be addressed because of its significance to all of those currently living on the Earth plane. It has to do with the area of addictions and how they affect the lives of millions throughout the world. Addictions are patterns of behavior that arise out of trauma and pain and affect daily life in many negative ways. When one experiences a very painful event or series of events, all levels of the organism are impacted strongly and directly. The entire electrical system governing the brain and central nervous system registers at a basic level the negative stimuli that have entered the forcefield. The emotional body reflects the initial shock with its attending anger, grief, or fear. Then the message is sent to all the cells of the body where the memory is stored until it is processed and released at a later date.

At the present time, there is little knowledge concerning the direct and immediate effect that stimuli from the physical world have upon all beings residing on the many planes of matter. Science is just beginning to understand and develop the concept of the unified field, which holds that everything in existence has a common matrix of experience. Recognition also is dawning that beings are not separate, isolated units unaffected by what transpires about them.

On the contrary, humans on the Earth plane are constantly changing, ever- moving fields of vibration, which reflect, refract and absorb the energy all about them. In the coming age, when humans will be able to see their own energy fields, as well as those of others, they will know how to cleanse and heal negative intrusions that affect them adversely. But since this ability is not widely known or practiced at the present time, most people are flying blind, as you would say in your world.

And so it is now that when one experiences a negative assault in word, deed or action, the effect is stored within cellular memory without the means for activating the process of release and healing. This negative energy is felt at the deepest level as a contraction of vital force, preventing the body from feeling the free flow of vibratory essences, which continuously circulate in our world. This contraction or blockage is then registered at the physical, emotional, or mental level as a nagging restlessness, anxiety or agitation that drives the individual to find an outlet, which will give relief.

This outlet is first reflected with an increase of hyperactivity in an area chosen by the individual. It can be work, play, drugs, alcohol, overeating, continuous talking, sex or any other series of self-destructive, repetitive actions that are used to assuage pain. One other component of an addiction is that the source of the pain is generally unknown or unrecognized by the individual who is in the throes of it. At this time, addictive behavior is at a very high level all over the world.

There are a number of reasons why this is so. The primary cause can be found in the many wars, violence and rampant materialism that have been predominant throughout the twentieth century. It is difficult to find anyone who has not been affected in one way or another by painful incidents in their lives. Also, cycles of 2,000 years, 5,000 years, 26,000 years, and 500,000 years are ending at this time.

At the conclusion of each of these time periods, the subconscious minds of the human race on the planet empty their storage banks of previous experience into the vibratory forcefield of the Earth. This is done so that humanity can clear the ledger and start afresh, as the saying goes. The release of this negative energy causes psychic pollution of major proportions, particularly for sensitive or receptive people. So, in some cases, the trauma or pain is not that of the person experiencing the addiction. The vibratory atmosphere is what is causing blockage at the cellular level.

To some reading these words, the idea of a vibratory field of negative, subconscious energy affecting the lives of human beings may seem unbelievable. But we ask that the reader attune to our words, for they are of extreme importance. So few people at the present time can recognize the vibratory fields about them that impact their physical, emotional and mental wellbeing. It is crucial that humans know, at a deep level, that they continuously project and receive vibratory influences from their world on an ongoing basis.

So, given this verity, what can one do to release and heal addictive behavior? It is easier than one who is suffering from the condition might think. First, one must be willing to look at one's behavior with a clear and discriminating eye. There has to be a desire for self-improvement with a willingness to make a firm commitment to it. Then one needs to become knowledgeable about what constitutes addictive behavior. Once all of these factors are in place, it is time for a courageous personal inventory of the individual's actions.

If it is recognized that an addiction is present, the remedy for release and healing needs to be devised. For instance, if a person is addicted to drug usage, treatment and rehabilitation can be found which, if entered into with firm intent, can bring success. Individuals and groups are excellent resources for support and encouragement during this period. So it is that one needs to seek out physical, emotional and psychological assistance in removing an addiction.

But there is an additional area, not as well recognized today. And that is the spiritual area. Because the pain causing the addiction ultimately resides at the level of spirit — either within the individual, or within the energy field, which he or she is presently occupying. At this point in time, little credence is given to the key role a person's energy field plays in treating addiction. So one has to learn the process of attuning to the realm of spirit. One can accomplish this by establishing a daily practice where time is set aside for silence, prayer and meditation, or connecting with nature. Accessing one's higher self as well as the spiritual guidance always available to all of us is needed for healing the entire system. Then ongoing adherence to spiritual practices will help keep the person centered and in balance.

Those individuals who are highly sensitive and are receiving an overload of negative psychic energy can stop this disturbance by recognizing what is happening to them and enclosing themselves within a radiating band of protective white light. This simple but effective visualization will end the penetration of unwanted vibrations. Then enhancing one's own energy field through thoughts of love will solidify and strengthen the personal aura immeasurably. For the strongest force in the universe is love. No darkness or negativity can exist where the love vibration is radiating steadily and continuously. So again and again we say to you, our dear friends on Earth, love and care for each other and the planet on which you reside. Then all will be well in the fields of matter!

# Developing
# Personal Power

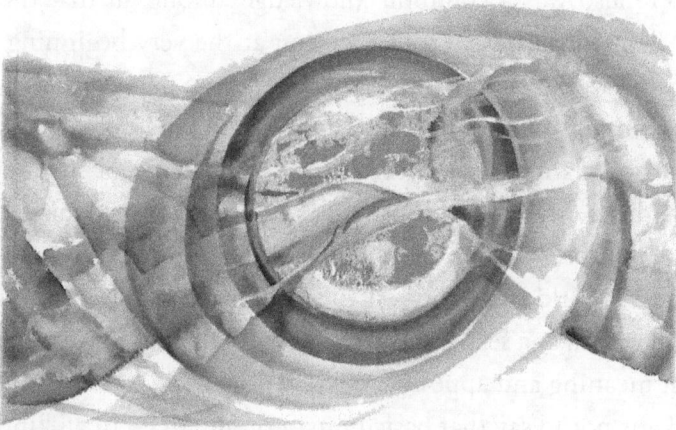

This period on the Earth is pivotal for the facing of issues that have long existed within those currently in incarnation. Now individuals must focus on developing their own personal power. It is a natural part of the evolutionary process of the soul to develop crystallized traits and characteristics that become solidified into rigid behavioral modes. This is as it always has been. For as a soul grows in certain life experiences, character traits become honed and established as part of the soul's matrix. After this is accomplished, the next step incorporates what has been learned into the very essence of the soul itself. The conclusion of this developmental process is the refining of character traits to remove the negative elements that have been acquired.

In earlier times, the process described above was known to all and incorporated into the education of ancient civilizations on the Earth. People knew of their spiritual origins and honored them in every area of their lives. Each day was set into motion with a brief period of prayer and attunement to the Divine Source. All knew that they were essences of spirit encased in a physical body which had the capability of accessing the higher dimensional realities at any given moment. They knew deep within their being that they were to develop and grow in spirit so that ultimately they could be reunited with the Source of All That Is.

There also was a common knowledge among all that they had a clearly defined purpose set into motion at the very beginning of creation. Every spirit was entrusted with a common goal — that of playing and creating in the various dimensions of the God Force for as long as the Creator planned existence. Think of this concept for a moment. What a difference it would make if humans could recognize that their primary purpose was to play and create. The priorities currently held in the western world would be very different indeed. The accumulation of material wealth as a security and status symbol would no longer hold its current meaning and appeal.

That is not to say that basic human productivity of all kinds would stop. On the contrary, the profusion of services and resources that are available today would still be in existence. But they would be initiated in a very different way. It would be recognized that the primary reason for bringing anything into existence would be for the sheer love of creating it and the great satisfaction that stems from this act. Inherent at a deep level in any creative process is the joy experienced in bringing into manifestation something that will be of service to others. Also there always exists a personal thrill in any creative act because one is reflecting back the most profound quality of the God Force.

At the present time on planet Earth, this ancient knowledge of the primary purpose of life must rise into the conscious awareness of the human race. Earth beings have a much greater capacity for expression than they are currently exhibiting. The brain, which is the servant of the soul's mind force, is using only one tenth of its capability, if that. Once the brain exercises one hundred percent of its intended expression, life will take on a full richness not comprehended in this day and age.

How will this expansion of the brain occur? When humans acknowledge and know at a deep level of their being that they have a spiritual base which is interconnected with the various dimensions and levels of the universe, the expansion within their cranial capacity will accelerate tremendously. An analogy exists right before one's very eyes in the computer, which was recently invented to reflect back to humans the reality of how their own brains operate and of what they are capable.

The abilities of today's computers seem wondrous indeed. But they are merely a dim reflection of what Earth beings will be able to perform once their brains can function in the manner for which they were created. One of the most important actions that can be performed in order to facilitate this expansion of brain capacity is entering into the meditative state and consciously attuning to higher dimensional realities. Meditation produces new centers in the brain and serves as a rewiring, as it were, for electrical pathways bringing in universal vibrations.

And so it is that this higher state has an important, concrete purpose in the evolutionary progress of the human species on the Earth. If one could think of himself or herself as a divine electrician who is continually upgrading the magnetic system within the brain so it can offer greatly increased knowledge and power, meditation would become a standard daily activity. It would be seen as a necessary form of physical exercise, as it were. So we ask that all who read these words reflect upon them at a deep level of being. For many, just the reading alone will activate a profound knowing which will assist them in incorporating meditation into the fabric of their lives. Are not these times in which you live most exciting indeed?

# Functioning in a Transpersonal Capacity

We now would like to speak to those of you who are finding the process of living increasingly difficult. You may feel isolated and cut off from what is familiar to you. You may also have a sense that you are losing all that is identifiable as you and that there is a vacuum at the core of your being. And it is so in certain ways. For the old personality that has been the persona with which you have experienced the world in this lifetime is fading away into nothingness. You will no longer need this ego self to separate and define who you are. You will become more and more soul-infused. All that has identified your human personality will no longer be important to your human expression.

One of the side effects of this developing condition is a strong sense of disconnectedness. You may find that you no longer relate to the vast majority of people in your life. Your activities in the outer world may be diminishing in amount and intensity. Many of the things you used to do seem no longer important or desirable. In fact, in some ways it may feel as if you were preparing yourself to die and leave this realm. However, this is not the case.

It is important that we speak about what is happening to all of you who are experiencing these inner changes. You need to have the information you require to ride out this crucial period of your life and progress into the work awaiting you. In a nutshell, as you would say, many of you are experiencing a death of the human personality as you move into the realm of your higher self. In order to be of service to humanity, you must die to your lower egoic self. If you do not, you cannot function in a transpersonal capacity on behalf of the Divine Plan.

What is meant by the term "transpersonal capacity"? One who lives transpersonally no longer experiences life in a mundane way. Instead, a higher spiritual purpose is recognized and followed at all times. The personal will is subordinated to the divine will of the Almighty Creator. And one is always connected to the higher powers of the universe on a regular and ongoing basis. The person has surrendered his or her lower egoic will to the higher divine will in all things.

Reflect upon what we are saying here. Do you not feel the truth of what we are describing? Because literally many of you are separating from the "you" which has been your vehicle for expression in this reality. And there exists no frame of reference for this experience in the western society of your day. The closest expression that describes what is happening to you is "the dark night of the soul".

Many have interpreted this phrase to mean a traumatic period in life characterized by intense suffering. But truly the dark night means much more than this. The dark night is the entire period in which the human personality is unaware of and disconnected from one's higher consciousness. As long as one exists in this state, it is as if one were seeing through a glass darkly. Plato's description of individuals in a cave seeing only with reflected light is the perfect depiction of this state. Only when the blinders come off and we see who we truly are, will we able to move into the realm of the transpersonal.

Then we will expand exponentially in all areas of our lives. We will know who we are and from whence we have come. We will see what our purpose in life is, and we will pursue it with single-minded focus and commitment. We will step into the role of a server of humanity and carry out our assignments with clarity of purpose. Our personal lives will change and transform. We will no longer gravitate to our earlier path of human expression but will strike out into fields of endeavor never before imagined.

But most important of all, our lives will take on a harmony and serenity unknown to us in the earlier days of our existence. Once we recognize what has happened to us, we will start to experience lives of spiritual direction and power. We truly will become instruments of the Creator always functioning for the higher good in whatever we do.

And so it is most important to recognize this step into the transpersonal realm and how it manifests in our lives. Never give in to fear or panic at the apparent dissolution of self. Let go of what you were and walk into the light of what you are becoming. All is in divine order and enveloped in the love of the Godhead.

# Personal Realization

Now the primary focus is one of personal realization and power. This is truly a time of separation. Some individuals will withstand the disintegrative elements of the incoming photonic particles and will use them for irradiation. While others will disintegrate at all levels because of the darkness and negativity held within.

In order to develop personal power it is essential that each individual becomes strong and self-sufficient in all ways. This is not to say that one cannot love and be loved by others with whom one is in relationship. But it is essential to remain personally whole within a strong integrity. To accomplish this requires deep personal awareness and intent. One must see oneself as part of a larger spiritual matrix or group — responsible and participating within the will of this group, in service of the Divine Oneness energy which permeates all matter.

Power is held within each being but is received also from a higher source. This power is always to be used to further the plan of Light and Love. Therefore, to be really attuned to power from a higher level, one must recognize the source of this energy and dedicate oneself to the higher good. In other words, one must live in a transcended state of purpose, intent and attunement. When this state is reached, one becomes a transcended being serving the Higher Will of the Divine. So personal power is truly far beyond what is currently believed from a limited egoic view.

During each of the four phases of the moon, it is important to see and feel this knowledge and start to function in a new and more inclusive manner, eschewing all personality, power-encoded actions. The old must be sloughed off like the skin of a snake and the new embraced.

The new species emerging will function totally from this power base. An example of this new level of functioning was modeled in the book The Tenth Insight, for those with the eyes of the soul to see. The main character in this tale saw the world of matter and the world of spirit and functioned as a bridge between both two realities — incorporating the elements of both in a unified purpose and task.

So in this time, meditate and reflect on these ideas. Look closely, if possible, at the truths found in The Tenth Insight. It presents a new human prototype for the future. To grow into this prototype, it is first essential to expand and develop a new concept of personal power. Once this concept is accepted and in place, there truly will be a new heaven and a new Earth on the planet.

The commitment to serve as a channel for the higher forces requires dedication and steadfastness in order to be able to receive and then transmit the higher octaves of light into the plane of matter. The physical vehicle must be strong and in balance. The emotions must be steady and in check. And the mind must be alert and free from debilitating ego involvement, both with oneself and with those in the sphere of influence in which the soul operates. So you see, it is not only an honor to serve in this capacity, but it is a great responsibility requiring dedication, self-discipline, and sacrifice.

What is life like for those souls who have agreed to serve in this capacity? First and foremost they are highly focused on the work at hand. They live normal lives that appear fairly mundane to those who know and observe them. Simplicity is the cornerstone of all that they are and do. Their continuous contact with universal forces brings an element of clarity into the perception of all that occurs around them. This clarity is sometimes so unsettling that they withdraw in order to maintain balance.

These dedicated souls have removed themselves from all issues that circulate within the culture in which they reside. No longer do the forces of the outer world affect them or motivate them to participate in worldly matters. Love, beauty, gentleness, and commitment to assist in bringing universal energies to the realm of matter is their primary focus. They live in a transcended state best expressed as "living in the world but not being of it". This is not to say that they do not have the normal human desires, needs and shortcomings. They are truly human in all ways. It is just that they have an added dimension that puts them in a slightly different category than those about them.

To serve in this capacity, one must recognize the choice and commitment he or she has made. Then one must organize life so that this path can be lived in the full richness of the human condition, participating, enjoying and even reveling in the many variations of spirit playing in the fields of matter. The single most important factor is that of recognition. These souls need to know, at a deep level of being, who they are and what they have come here to do. Then they have to possess the personal power required to manifest the service they are here to perform.

The final criterion is that of fusion. These souls must never feel or act as separate from their world and everything in it. This would be a serious flaw and negation of all they are. There also can be no sense or feeling of superiority on a personal level. Humility is one of the primary qualities that these souls must possess. For they are just one tile in the mosaic of Divine Oneness, serving in a specific capacity, just as every other soul serves in a designated way in the Divine Plan. Reflect on these words. They hold great significance for all.

It is important that one see the way in which the dictates of spirit are unfolding and accept them as good. All of life is a series of choices. Each individual living on the Earth plane is faced with many probable futures predicated on a wide variety of life situations and relationships. And since very few have learned how to access their inner state of spiritual wisdom, the choices they make are often from their human egoic self. But this is for the highest good, for only through trial and error will the realization grow that true wisdom comes from the inner spiritual center of the being.

And so it is that human life on this planet ebbs and flows in the divine spiral of the Creator — failing and stumbling, learning and growing. In this beautiful dance of spirit, humanity never stops persevering upward, ever upward, toward the goal of reunion with All That Is. Every thought that is made, every action that is taken contributes to the expansion of consciousness, no matter how it may look to an observer. This is why one must always believe in the innate goodness of choices that anyone may make. Everything contributes to the growth of wisdom, no matter how negative it might appear.

When one reaches the acceptance of what we have just said here, a state of peace and faith is gained for all that unfolds in life. No guilt, regret, pain or dismay can enter this state and destroy its inner serenity. All is truly in divine order and progressing upward in the spiral of the One. Whoever is in this state knows that he or she is a spark of the Creator, here to play and grow and learn in the fields of matter. Can the readers of these words not feel the comfort and power in what we say here? This is your birthright, children of Earth. It is a beautiful one indeed. Is it not?

# *The Divine Dance –*
# *An Ebb And*
# *Flow Of Energy*

One of the most important abilities a human being can have today is that of attunement — attunement to one's own body and its needs, attunement to the people and conditions that exist around one, and finally attunement to the vibratory energy of spirit. We ask all of those reading these words to set aside a period each day for a quiet connection to spirit. This inner checking for what the appropriate activity is at the right time will become essential for the humans of the future.

For you see, ultimately all that exists is contained in vibratory waves of subatomic particles. These particles are imbued with the mind force of the Ultimate. They have intelligence at the deepest level of being. Everything exists and lives in this great cosmic soup. To be aware of this fact and to consistently attune to this energy source which arises throughout the universe, both within and without, is the goal for which we all are striving. One becomes an enlightened being when one is able to attune to this energy force. We call it enlightened because the basis of vibratory energy is light.

## Attunement

Today, at this point in time on the Earth, there is much discussion about being enlightened. Most of the interpretations of the state of enlightenment speak to a high spiritual state achieved by a very few after much training and austerity. This perception of enlightenment is somewhat flawed and expresses the human egoic view.

True enlightenment is a simple but very profound process. It merely entails recognizing that all of existence is found within a subatomic vibratory field. To know this, and then to attune to its energy emanations, brings increased light into the physical and electromagnetic bodies of a human being. This increased enlightenment raises the vibratory wavelength and increases awareness and functioning exponentially.

As we have said, many on the Earth plane have been looking at the issue of how to respond when they are in the company of someone who is acting in a manner which affects them adversely. This is a most important question and one that is coming to the forefront of human behavior. For a long period of time, humans have tolerated or fought against the hurtful actions of others. There have been two primary responses used in most interpersonal relationships. To stay connected to the person or situation, accepting the negative behavior, or to stay connected and fight to attain supremacy has been the predominant mode of human interaction down through the ages.

But there is a new way that is evolving into prominence. And it has to do with the concept discussed above. As more and more people become enlightened, they are functioning at a level of energy attunement instead of the level of the personality or ego. Therefore, when they find themselves in a situation where discordant energy waves are prevalent, they feel such intense discomfort that they have to leave the influence of that forcefield in order to maintain equilibrium and balance.

At a subatomic level, they are in great distress until they relieve themselves of the pressure of the situation. Instead of engaging with the discordant energy by passively accepting it or fighting it, they disengage and leave it with no judgement. The energy is just unsuitable to their vibratory wavelength. Those that remain in the situation are doing so because the discomfort has not reached the intolerable stage for them. It is as simple as that.

So we ask the reader not to feel any guilt or concern about your actions when you remove yourself from discordant people or situations. It is purely a matter of the impact that the prevailing energy has upon you and nothing more. One can simply say, "I cannot remain. The energy being projected here is affecting me adversely. I need to remove myself." If all of the beings on Earth were able to function in this manner, there truly would be a new heaven and a new Earth.

We ask that you not be discouraged when you waver and return to earthly practices. It is to be expected within the vibrational field you inhabit. The key factor here is to recognize the pull of matter and its effect on human behavior. Keep attuning to the vibratory impulses that you receive continually. Flow with them minute by minute and you will be in harmony and balance. For total harmony and balance is a state of stasis and nonaction that is uncreative because of its equilibrium. All beings exist in an evermoving field of balance to imbalance back to balance again. This is the divine dance of the universe as seen in the Hindu depiction of the dance of Shiva. It is most important that you know and recognize this fundamental truth.

How does this information apply to one's life on a daily basis? It is very simple. You, as an individual unit within the creation of the Divine, will be involved in the very same dance that exists throughout the many universes of time and space. You will ebb and flow from balance to imbalance. Then you will adjust and return to balance again. Without this process so basic to the state of being and creating, no existence within the realms of matter would be possible.

So honor this process. Do not judge yourself negatively when the periods of imbalance occur. Know them for what they are. It is the creative friction required for the ongoing emergence of all that lives and moves and has its being within the greater framework of the universe. Honor this energy pattern. Play with it. Recognize that when you are out of balance it is because you are about to move back into a state of equilibrium, which is an upward step on the spiral of life. The imbalance is the springboard for the necessary growth and expansion of beings within the energy field of All That Is.

We ask that you reflect deeply on these words and the truths that they hold. In order to truly serve, one must know the basics, as it is said in your culture. What we are presenting here are the basics at a much deeper and more profound level of functioning. When you learn to recognize and adhere to this ancient knowledge, life will take on a totally new dimension for you.

You will see yourself as a unit of matter functioning within a greater energy matrix. That field then is part of an even greater field, which is part of an even greater field and so on into infinity. Your major responsibility is to exist and create within this context, nothing more. The vibrational attunement of these creative acts will determine your place within the fields of matter. It is most simple, is it not?

The time of Great Awakening is approaching closer ever closer. Continue to prepare yourself in all ways. The single most important aspect of this preparation is the inner attunement to the universal rhythms ever present on a minute-by-minute basis. True impeccability is found only in perfected attunement. Reflect on this idea, for it contains great power. To be in harmony with the universal flow of vibrational energy is the ultimate goal of every conscious being existing throughout the many universes of the Creator. What is it that allows and enhances this attunement, and what detracts from this process of merger and union? These are the questions we would like to address with you now.

All that exists in the world of spirit and matter flows in waves of subatomic particles in a beautiful undulating rhythm, wafting in a continuous flow throughout time and space. This everlasting continuum is part and parcel of the field in which it is found. It is most important to recognize first and foremost that we are immersed in a larger field of spirit-matter that flows in, around and through us.

This field has ever-changing properties that, if seen, would reflect and refract the entire spectrum of light and color in an irradiating kaleidoscope of great beauty and power. In time all conscious beings will know this and see the varying spectrum with their sensing and viewing apparatus. They will then adjust and attune their own energy field so that it is in alignment with the greater energy within which they live and have their being.

Every interpersonal dynamic between humans on the Earth at this time is a reflection of two things – a greater energy field and their own personal energy field. Negative actions and intentions carry a lower and more dense vibration and radiation, which has the effect of slowing down the wave particles within the field at large. When this occurs, there is an immediate reduction in light and sound. The best example that can be given is that of a tape or record that has been slowed down in megahertz. The effect upon the listeners is that of agitation, irritation, and discomfort.

That is why, at the present time on Earth, there is such an emphasis on the upgrading of human behavior and the improvement of interpersonal relationships. Negative interaction is a pure and simple matter of adversely affecting energy at its most basic level. The resulting effect of this discordance is a diminution of light.

Presently on planet Earth, certain negative energy-reducing dynamics are being highlighted for elimination from the human condition. Anger, control, domination and manipulation have been deeply ingrained in the human psyche for eons on this planet and throughout the many universes of time and space. They have been the staples of human interaction. They reflected the lower vibrational frequency that was the norm for behavior everywhere. Most human interaction carries continuous elements of these four behavioral modes. But now, beings on Earth are in the vanguard of change that is radiating throughout time and space.

A new species of human is being birthed. This new species will function at a higher vibrational frequency. Its prevailing mode of interpersonal interaction will be based on love, respect, truth and attunement. These negative aspects of human behavior that have been in existence for eons will be recognized as undesirable at a basic level of interaction and will be dropped from the lexicon of acceptable human behavior. The knowledge gained through many existences will sink into the humus of soul knowing and will exist only at the subconscious level, surfacing for consideration when necessary.

Meditate and reflect on these concepts. They are of great significance at this time to all those in human incarnation. As the awareness of this information grows and human nature starts to change, there will be an increase in the energy field of light and vibration that truly will create a new heaven and a new Earth on your planet. This new energy field will serve as the matrix for the new species that is waiting for its time to experience life on your planet. Without the appropriate vibratory field, this species cannot come into being. So the work that is done now has major significance in the overall unfolding of the Divine Plan.

# Earth as a Laboratory for Growth

In the future there will be small segments of people around the world who will live and prosper as remnant groups carrying forth the ideas and values which will birth a new heaven and a new Earth. This process has occurred throughout the history of humankind and will continue to happen again in the future. A very long cycle in the evolution of the human species is ending. Much has been experienced and much has been learned by the souls who have incarnated on this plane of matter down through the eons.

Earth has served as a wonderful laboratory or teaching environment for evolving souls returning on the path to reunion with the Source. For this is the primary process which unfolds throughout the many universes of time and space. All that emerges in the affairs of conscious beings is held within this basic construct. The goal of each soul is to experience and play in the fields of matter and finally return to the Godhead as realized beings who know what it means to combine all the elements of spirit and matter into a unified whole.

It is time for this basic awareness to permeate the ethers and atmosphere of Earth. Earth beings can begin to claim their rightful heritage. In the coming ages the Children of Light, as Earth beings will be called, will ascend and move out into the many galaxies of the universe. They will seed new civilizations that in turn will offer a matrix within which the Godhead can play, create and just be. So now we ask that you see what your primary role is. It is time for you to recognize and own your power. Then you will be able to participate in this divine dance which is the true unfolding of All That Is. So reflect on these words. They have great significance for you at many levels.

We also ask that you meditate upon the world about you. For it is a basic truth that the physical environment must be in harmony with the activities performed within it. Everything that manifests on the realm of three-dimensional matter must reflect the energy field that is creating it. All one has to do to determine what exists at the level of spirit is to observe what is in existence in the physical reality. With this thought in mind, we ask that those of you reading these words look at your house and physical surroundings. They mirror with great accuracy the spiritual energies from which they have emanated.

There are many days of great beauty in the natural world on your planet. On some days that occur with regularity, the light of spirit shines at a higher octave than on other days. It seems as if a quietude or stillness has settled on the land, and all is hushed. Watch these days and feel the intensity of their vibrational content. These days are truly a gift from All That Is. They are meant to be a time of healing and expanded awareness for all conscious beings. This time is pregnant with possibility awaiting manifestation.

Tune into the spiritual content of the energy all about you. Observe what you learn and experience. Note it at the end of the day. Then you will be able to recognize this very special energy when it appears the next time. The best way to describe what is occurring is to remember the beauty, stillness and freshness that one may experience after a storm. The sense of renewal and joyful peace is very strong.

Watch all your actions and reactions as you move within this energy field. You will notice that there is expanded awareness of everyone and everything about you. At this point in time, seeds for the future can be planted in this fertile wave of energy undulating throughout the universe. The best depiction of this state can be found in the book of Genesis, where God rested on the seventh day of creation. The sense of peace and fulfillment that comes from experiencing all the many facets of existence brings an awareness, satisfaction and knowledge of what it is to play in the fields of matter. Dance in the energy field on these days and return in the evening to reflect upon what you have learned.

On nights when the moon is full, there is also a very special energy abroad in the land permeating all that exists on the plane of matter. Energy particles of the finest substance found at the level of spirit infiltrate the three-dimensional world. This energy illuminates and irradiates all that is on the Earth plane. It contains the awareness of knowledge to be acquired during the first phase of each moon cycle. For each cycle has a life lesson to be learned and absorbed.

This awareness was known in early societies all over the Earth. Rituals and religious practices centered on the moon, and people were able to recognize and respond to the teaching emanating from the moon. In the future, there will be a return to this ancient knowledge with its attending rituals. And humans on the Earth plane will again absorb the moon's vibrations into the deepest level of their being.

## Our Body's Vibratory Field

The practices of yoga and Reiki are ancient rituals that have been used as means to access the higher dimensional realms for a very long time indeed. Yoga is highly beneficial to the physical body in many ways. It tones and stretches the body to keep it limber and supple. It connects the nervous and electrical system of the body to its outer etheric casing, which is necessary for the continual alignment that the body requires. People who desire good health and attunement to the higher realms have always performed some type of yogic practice.

It is extremely important that yoga, which unites the physical body with its electrical and etheric sheaths, be practiced on a regular and ongoing basis. For the electromagnetic forcefield of the Earth has weakened considerably in the last thousand years, affecting directly the ability of the human body to sustain itself for a long period of time. In order to strengthen and counteract the planet's weaker electrical field, humans must take strong extra measures to enhance their physical vehicles. Bodies are indeed vehicles in that they are the transportation for the soul. Care of the body is a sacred duty and trust.

This is why the many sciences that enhance the well being of the body are moving into the forefront of human awareness. It is known at a deep inner level that physical bodies must be prepared for the great shift in consciousness which is about to occur. Therefore Earth beings must start to see themselves in a new and totally different vein. They must come to recognize that they are souls of vibratory light which inhabit a physical body in order to experience and impact matter. As part of their basic equipment, they are endowed with mental and emotional bodies, which assist the soul and the physical form in every aspect of its life.

The newly emerging field of energetics will be of great assistance in bringing awareness of their true state to those living on the Earth. When one sees oneself as a being composed primarily of vibratory energy particles interacting in a specific way, human consciousness will take a giant step forward in its evolutionary journey back to the Source of All That Is. Then and only then will the science of energetics become widely used in everyday existence. Humans will invent many new techniques that will diagnose, monitor, and treat the human body as a vibratory field first and foremost. Because of this recognition, it will be possible to counteract the lowered electromagnetic energy of the planet by generating what the body needs through methods not yet in existence at this time.

So one of the most important things that one can do is to attune to one's own energy field and experience what it feels like in a direct and measurable way. The ancient spiritual exercise of meditation is the primary practice that will bring about this knowledge. When one quiets the physical, emotional, and mental bodies, it is possible to hear and feel the vibratory waves that flow continuously within the human matrix. Then the individual can know at a deep level that he or she is connected to and part of a great body of energy, ever-present and always self-sustaining.

Therefore the most important request that we can make at this time is that you adopt a personal practice daily of quieting and attuning to your own personal energy and then the energy of the world about you. If this request is honored, you will start to experience transformation in a profound manner indeed. Meditation opens a door to higher dimensional realities which, when known, changes forever one's view of oneself and the world in which one lives. Then and only then can one start to play with energy in the way it was truly intended.

The Divine Creator meant that all beings should possess the capacity to create fully in the fields of both spirit and matter. In order to utilize that gift, one must know clearly who one is and from whence one has come. We are all offspring of the Primal Source, which intended from the beginning that we would have the power to create and enjoy the many worlds of time and space. Now at the end of this great century of learning and change, those living on planet Earth are ready to take a giant step forward on the path of return. Make this step with the beauty, power and grace which always has been your birthright. A new time of light and love is fast approaching. Can you not feel the wonder of what is almost upon you? Go within and you will know!

# Triangulation

Now we would like to talk with you about the concept of triangulation, which has been such a necessary foundation for this transmission process. During the past two thousand Earth years of the Piscean vibration, the mode of receiving information from the realm of spirit had a clearly recognizable context. One individual, group, church or government brought forth knowledge that was passed from the realm of spirit into human consciousness. In a few instances, there were awareness and honoring of the source from whence it came. But in most cases, there was little recognition of the spiritual imprinting that was creating the blueprint to be manifested on the Earth plane. The information came forth and was accepted by the populace as routine human expression.

But the Earth is moving into a new age, one called Aquarian in astrological circles. One of the primary characteristics of this two-thousand-year cycle will be the close interaction between the realms of spirit and matter. It will come to be recognized widely that all that is brought into existence on Earth originates from a spiritual idea or blueprint, which is then projected onto the Earth plane for creation.

So one of the most important abilities for humans living on planet Earth will be that of attunement to the higher dimensions. The methods for accomplishing this ability will be taught at an early age as part of the educational program for the young. All conscious beings on this planet will eventually be aware of and functioning within the context of a greatly expanded bond with their spiritual source.

A primary truth that will be recognized is the importance of energy in all its manifestations. Humans will be able to see energy fields and recognize the quality of the molecular world about them. They will come to know that everything that manifests on the plane of form comes from an energy field at a higher level. This imprint enters human consciousness and appears at the level of matter, reflecting the channel through which it came. The energy field of the receiving entity or group will color significantly the creative result.

So the idea of triangular foundations of energy for creative expression will come into existence. Energy that manifests within a triangular field is the most harmonious and enduring for those living on planet Earth. The Earth chain existed within a universe whose primary mode of expression was triangular before this current universe came into being. It is now time for this primeval experience to be incorporated into all levels of life on Earth. It will bring peace and harmony, which will ground this new age of truth and light. It will soon be known that creation which is successful must come through a certain framework — that of the base of three.

Triangulation is a much more profound process than most of you can envision at this time. Triangulation can occur in many different ways. Three humans can come together and offer the grounding that is required for the creative process. And those three humans can vary and change depending on the circumstances. But entities from the realm of spirit also can be called upon for assistance.

Triangulation is purely an energy construct and nothing more. Since this is so, those living in matter and those residing within the many realms of spirit can supply the energy. Because all that exists is imbued with the divine essence of the Creator, therefore any source can be called upon to build the foundation for a creative endeavor.

This process has been used down through the ages by many cultures as a beginning ritual for significant actions that were of benefit to the whole. But every endeavor of body, mind and spirit will need a triangulation imprint from this point forward for success. Therefore you will see emerging throughout the Earth a growing awareness of triangulation coupled with specific practices in all areas of life.

You ask how this triangulation will manifest in actual reality. For some time, the triangulation process will be unconscious except in a very few cases. But as the awareness surfaces throughout humankind on the planet, like a yeast raising bread, more and more individuals will begin each activity of any import with a triangulation ritual that will become almost automatic over time. The reason that triangulation will be a basic concept used by all is that there will be a growing knowledge in the future about energy with its varying properties and manifestations.

All that exists throughout the many universes of time and space has, at its base, energy particles imbued with the spirit force of the Creator. Therefore to really understand and master the world in which one lives, one must recognize this fundamental truth. Everything that lives in manifested form has at the core of its essence a universal energy, which contains the divine creative force. For this reason, the development of science in the past three centuries has been a key step in the progress of human beings on the planet. Science is proving to a materially oriented western world that energy does exist and can be measured in its many facets.

However, the step that has not been taken but which is coming closer, ever closer, is the recognition that this energy has been created by a divine source. Once this truth is known widely, there will be a shift of immense proportions on planet Earth. To know that everything that exists has its own energy field, which contains certain specific properties, will raise consciousness onto a new multidimensional level. This knowledge will transform the world of those living on the Earth plane dramatically. The structure, function, health and longevity of the human body will be greatly changed for the better. New inventions in all areas of life will be forthcoming which will raise the standard of life all over the Earth.

Let us take transportation as an example. To recognize that the human body is comprised of an electromagnetic forcefield will revolutionize the way in which life is viewed. The next step will be to explore the manner in which the human body interacts with the energy fields about it. Not long after that, discoveries will come which will relate the movement of the body to the many energy fields surrounding it.

As new principles of dynamic propulsion are discovered which have at their base an energy-related construct, new methods of transporting the human body will appear and be put into daily use. It will be learned that the energy molecules of the human body can be dissembled and then reassembled at another location anywhere in the universe. Also, new types of vehicles will be invented which will transport individuals at warp speed to their selected destinations with a minimum of time and discomfort.

So one can see the great importance of the growing awareness of energy and how it holds and sustains every living thing. Another example of an area that will be totally transformed is that of health. To recognize that the human body is an energy field will change totally the manner in which it is treated for illness.

The energy field of the body will be used as the basis for diagnosis and treatment. And the treatment will include methods that will affect positively the body's electrical circuitry. That is not to say that physical treatment will disappear, for that will not be the case. But the primary diagnosis will be of the electromagnetic energy of the sick person, and then physical body treatment will be devised based on the needs of the forcefield.

Energy triangulation will be a basic component of the newly emerging energy-related science. For as the many principles of energy are discovered, so also will the properties of energy be revealed. Once these are known, the entire study of triangulation will naturally follow, since triangulation is inherent in all energy manifestation. So those individuals who are pioneering the concepts of energetics and triangulation are performing a most important service for humankind. They will be the trailblazers for the commonly accepted truths of the future.

We ask that those individuals who feel attracted to any aspect of energetics hold true to their course. It only takes a certain number believing and following an idea for it to take hold and register in the mass consciousness of the planet. When this awareness is fully operational in the world, a new day of love and peace will dawn, pure and sweet for all those residing on the Earth.

# The Great Awakening – a Period of Transition

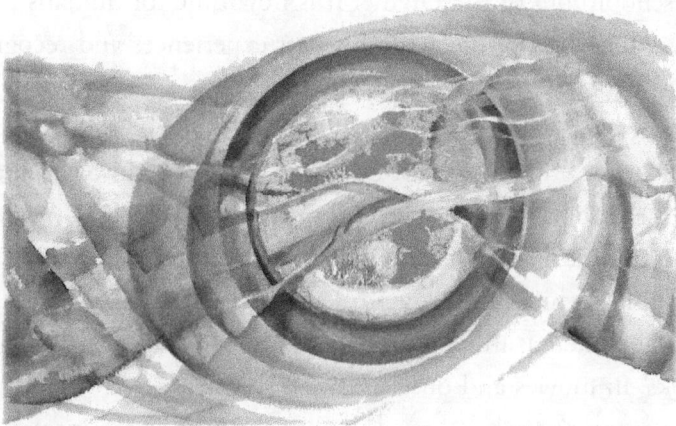

The winds of change are blowing strongly, symbolizing the movement that is beginning to stir all over the Earth. These winds will bring momentous events as they pick up and increase in the days, months, and years ahead. Wind is spirit in manifested form, cleansing and clearing old energy patterns that need to be moved out of existence. The Earth is truly in the midst of the Great Purification that the Native American peoples have foretold for centuries. The old era is ending.

There should be much appreciation for all the life experiences and learning that this age has supplied. It has not been easy to bring forth the difficult lessons of dense matter manifestation which the guiding spirits of this period have been assigned. Rather than reject all the many important lessons of the past, the new species will honor and remember the travail that was lived by their ancestors in order to provide the humus for the new turn of the spiral.

The process that has been unfolding has been that of involution and evolution. Spirit has come into matter down to its lowest level and now is starting the return back to the higher planes with the complete knowledge of what it means to live on the third-dimensional level. Much suffering has occurred in this learning process, which has served as the schoolroom of the Divine. It is now time for humans to release the pain and fears connected with past experiences and recognize the inherent benefits that have accrued from them. One can only become aware when one undergoes something directly. The knowledge of what it means to be human can not be learned secondhand or from afar.

Those who have been incarnating on the Earth plane down through the eons of time have played many different roles as they moved through the lifetimes, which molded and developed their soul essences. In this present age, there is much that triggers the memories of these lifetimes in books, in movies and on television. Through these different means, ancient memories are activated so that they can come into awareness, at least on the subtle level. For at the end of each age or period of manifestation, there is an accumulation of knowledge somewhere at the conscious level of each individual as to what has been his or her path through the fields of matter.

It is most important that this accumulation of acquired experience sinks into the humus of the soul so that the lessons learned become part of the soul matrix, to be drawn upon in future lives as innate knowing. And yet the word "future" is somewhat misleading since there is no past, present or future in the world of spirit or matter. All that exists is occurring in the Ever-present Now. We know that this is a difficult concept to grasp, but we would like to bring it forth for the consideration of all those who read these words.

At the start of each period of creation, life begins in its entirety and unfolds as a complete and whole picture, reflecting back all that makes up the mosaic of the Dance of the Creator. Part of the distortion experienced on the Earth plane is that everything that occurs seems to spring forth from a progression of time, which comes from the past, exists, and then moves into the future. Nothing could be further from the truth. Just as each cell contains the hologram of the entire body, so also the entire span of creation is reflected in its entirety from the moment of its birth.

Only when souls experience other dimensional levels will the realization of what is being said here come into awareness. The reason that we speak of this now is to bring forth the reality of the great diversity that exists within the universes of time and space. As the consciousness of human beings expands to reflect the many levels of Prime Creator, there will be a corresponding vibratory pulsation that will radiate throughout the many worlds.

This beam of spiritual light will uplift and irradiate every realm into which it shines. This is the true purpose of creation — to infuse each area of the universe with the light of the Holy Spirit. When everything that is reflects totally the essence of the Creator, then the purpose for the Divine Play of the Godhead is finished, at least for this period of manifestation.

All human beings currently living on planet Earth have committed themselves to an expansion of consciousness of major proportions. One of the key elements of this expansion is the ability to see themselves as multidimensional beings functioning in many different realms. In the next two thousand years of Earth time, all inhabitants of the planet will know who they are and from whence they have come. They will see themselves as galactic citizens linked to countless others throughout all of the universes existing within God's creation.

They will look back at this span of Earth time and call it the period of Great Awakening. For the capacity of humankind is about to take a giant step forward on the evolutionary spiral of life. Expanded powers and awareness will be the norm for all. It is only a short time, in the overall scheme of things, before this awakening will occur. The Earth is moving through a photonic belt of super radiation that will transform all life on the planet. It will cause deep growth in the powers and abilities of all humans who can live within the intensity of the approaching forcefield.

That is why we have mentioned many times the necessity for preparation. The physical body must be strengthened and at the same time refined in order to be compatible with the photonic particles that will penetrate everything that exists, whether in animate or inanimate form. Physical bodies must be readied electrically in order to absorb the increased radiation. This can best be accomplished by first expanding the brain-mind to withstand the increased force being directed to it. Also the etheric or electrical body surrounding the physical body needs to be supported to process the overload which will be moving into its system.

How this can be done is the question. Again we reiterate — meditation, expanding sensory awareness, and ingesting flower essences that work on the body's electrical system. These three are the means by which the body and mind will be able to tolerate and grow in the coming times of increased photonic radiation.

## The Third Dimensional World

We acknowledge and recognize how intense the pull of materiality is for all of you. It is the great challenge which Earth beings face as they proceed to create a balance between spirit and matter or form. The gravitational pull of the magnetic force field of the planet is necessary to its very existence. But this attraction provides a serious challenge to the task of spiritualizing all that exists on this plane.

We know that many of you feel the distraction and drain of the earthly demands on your time and energy. One of the great tests that all humans must pass is the ability to extract themselves from the gravitational pull of form so they can keep their connection to the higher realms and dimensions alive. But it is important at the same time to honor the plane on which you reside, all the while seeing clearly the nature of life in the third dimension. For, you see, you are here to irradiate all aspects of matter with the uplifting elements of spirit. In order for full well-being to exist, there has to be a balance between the two.

Those people immersed totally in materiality will not experience much inner conflict. What exists for them is a sense of deep hollowness which they constantly attempt to fill with more activity and more forays into all aspects of the material experience — none of which are satisfying at a deeper level of being. Others see the elements of spirit, although through a glass darkly. The discomfort of being immersed in the world of form can be excruciatingly painful for them. It is akin to seeing a beautiful land just out of reach in the distance and not being able to move towards it.

But there is such a simple way out of this dilemma of duality. The answer lies in just recognizing your world for what it is and knowing what you are here to do at this time. All humans on Earth live and move and have their being in the world of third-dimensional form. It is a great honor to be selected to live at this level, since Earth is one of the laboratories of the universe. To be able to fuse spirit with matter is one of the ultimate goals of the Divine Plan that is unfolding.

So recognize matter for what it is — the result of the creativity of spirit reduced to concrete form. You are here to accomplish the union of the two opposites. So do not dishonor or deny the importance of the realm in which you live. At the same time, do not allow the needs and desires of the material to be the motivating factor for how you live your life.

The connection to spirit must be the overriding director of at all times. The higher self of each person always must be the guiding force. Priorities must place the needs of spirit equal to the needs of form.

If this balance is in place, the individual continually will feel a sense of peace and harmony no matter what the outer circumstances of the life may be.

There will always be those people and situations which will attempt to pull the person on the spiritual path away from a healthy and balanced focus. And so it is that one must develop a firm commitment and resolve, which never wavers when one is pulled back into materiality. Two abilities are essential in preventing this from happening. First is clear-eyed discrimination, which is constantly watchful for intrusions that attempt to change one's course. And the other is strength of will, which girds the individual to maintain the necessary balance that life on the planet requires.

Reflect on these two qualities of discrimination and will. What does it take to recognize when balance is being lost? How does one identify the cause? It takes the clear eye of the eagle, which spares no one, not even the self. What is required to get back into balance, with the attending harmony it provides? A powerful will is the only solution to the dilemma. This divine characteristic of the Creator is the ultimate goal of spiritual development. Once one has honed a will of great strength which is in constant attunement to Divine Will, all the problems of existence fall away.

The human egoic personality is no longer the director of the life. The higher self is totally in charge, and the human personality serves as an implementer and nothing more. So one of the most important activities is connecting on a regular basis with one's higher self. That is why the practice of meditation has been reintroduced into the mainstream of human life. It is the most powerful and effective channel to the soul or higher self of each and every individual. When one recognizes and acknowledges at a basic level of being that one is a spirit inhabiting a physical body, matter will have lost its power to confuse and deter one from life's purpose.

So meditate daily, twice if possible. Always address every request for your time with the clear and discriminating eye of the higher self. The soul knows what types of activities are in your best interest and what are not. It also will not accede to others' views of what is best for you. It will set its course with Divine Love and Will as the two guiding forces of life. They will serve as stalwart pillars, supporting and sustaining you throughout the many twists and turns that life takes on the journey back to union with the Creator.

## Powers of Adjustment

There are days that epitomize all that is fair and good in the world of the Divine. When they occur, it is particularly beneficial to pause and experience the harmonious energy wafting and dancing throughout your world. These periods are to be savored and recognized as previews of the times to come. When planet Earth is finally restored to its earlier state, these days will be commonplace. The weather and atmospheric conditions reflect directly the state of overall health of the many kinds of beings residing within its sphere. This knowledge is a helpful barometer for assessing the degree of attunement that exists at any given time.

One need only look at the current weather and atmospheric conditions on your planet to see at a glance the extreme lack of equilibrium that has developed. As this instability worsens, counterbalancing forces will be brought into motion to correct the situation. These mighty powers exist throughout the many universes of time and space. They have the responsibility of adjustment for any person, situation or condition that has strayed from the golden mean. These forces have been depicted in all cultures in varying ways. In ancient Mu they were worshiped as the Four Primary Forces and their symbol was the equal-sided cross which has been found in every culture since that time.

It is the divine responsibility of these powers to work on behalf of All That Is to hold the framework of the universe in a state of an ever-evolving spiral motion. These forces deal with anything that impedes or holds this motion back. That is why your Earth is going through ever-worsening weather and climatic conditions. The actions of humankind have strayed so far from the golden mean of spirit that the corrective forces are coming into full sway. Their task is to preserve the Earth for future generations that are waiting in the wings, as it were, for their opportunity to experience the Earth forcefield as a school for spiritualizing matter.

These corrective powers can be quite severe if the situation warrants; and at this point in time it definitely does. So start to prepare yourself for what is to come. The first step is to acknowledge that this adjustment process is truly necessary. The second step is to be observant and watchful as to the development the course of correction will take. The third step is to attune to the universal energies which will provide the information you will require in order to ride the waves that will be breaking against the shores of your world with ever-increasing severity and violence.

The important thing for you to remember is that all is well and in divine order in the many universes of the Prime Creator. Even though to normal observation it would appear that there is much to sorrow over in the affairs of humans on Earth, that simply is not the case. All manifested matter is somewhere in the process of being created, growing or dying. Creation comes out of a state of chaos and initially from the void of all possibility, which appears to many as a most frightening state indeed. However, there is comfort in the process of growing, since development has an aspect of abundance and enthusiasm to it.

But the most demanding and trying part is that of dissolution or dying. There is much pain and loss connected to this segment of the human experience. But it is necessary in order to clear the way and prepare for the next level of manifestation in the Divine Plan. This last state is where the planet Earth is right now. So honor, accept, flow and dance with the energy that exists all about you. Is it not wonderful to experience all manner of creation?

# A Time of Change

All of the events leading to the Great Change are accelerating from this time forward. As the world moved into the pivotal year of 1998, everyone throughout the Earth began to know at a deep level of being that life on this planet is being transformed right before his or her very eyes. It is important that those in incarnation understand at a soul level what is transpiring now and for what reason.

We have given you information about the beginnings of human existence on this planet and the growth and development of the life force down through the ages. We also have told you about the coming age, featuring in detail what the new species and their skills and abilities will be.

Now we would like to speak rather extensively about these days in which you currently live. Much has been written earlier about the end times of this great age of Pisces. It was known at the highest dimensional levels that this current two-thousand-year period would be one of preparation for the emergence of a new species, which would lead the Earth back to reunion with the Great Creative Force of the universe. For a long span of time, those incarnating on this planet have been sinking deeper, ever deeper, into form. This was necessary so that they could know at a basic level of their essence what the properties of matter felt like in every way.

The many painful experiences of these past two millennia have been perfect and necessary for the unfolding of the Divine Plan. It is most important to see this truth and honor it even at the personal level. All that has been difficult and hurtful in the past has helped bring human consciousness to its present state of experiential wisdom and knowing. So rejoice and recognize that those residing on the Earth have been participating in a school of discipline forming them into the beings of great beauty that they are today. They need to understand what has happened so that they can develop wisdom for their future endeavors.

The receiving of transmissions from the realm of spirit is an effort of great beauty. This phenomenon of a co-creative relationship between a human and entities residing upon other dimensional levels has occurred throughout time in every area of the universe in which you reside. At key junctures, it has been important that communication take place in order for significant information to come directly and clearly. All of life in physical and spiritual form evolves around ever-increasing awareness and consciousness. It is as simple as that. We are here to grow and create — nothing more. So the transmission of information to expand the development of the individual and group soul is most important, particularly now.

This period of time on planet Earth is one of extreme significance for all those beings currently in human incarnation. There is not one entity living who has not chosen to be here for the Great Step Forward which is about to occur. So to anyone questioning whether he or she wants to move into the end times of this age, we would simply say this: Wake up and remember what you decided before you took on your current human role. There were many souls literally waiting in the wings (was that not a good play on words?) to be selected by the higher powers for an assignment on Earth. Each and every human being living at this time was honored to be selected. So accept this fact with humility and reverence for whom you are and what you have to give towards this coming divine adventure.

For, you see, all of life is a great gift from the Creator. This gift must be appreciated with every moment and every breath. Without the Great Primary Principle, sustaining and creating everything that exists throughout time and space, there would be nothing. So honor the Creator each day by valuing and respecting first yourself and then all those who inhabit your world in every form.

There are many beings living on the Earth that you do not see. They exist on a different vibrational level and so are not visible to humans who are seeing only three-dimensionally. Down though the ages, some individuals have moved into multidimensionality and have recognized the presence of these entities. Hence there have been many stories about fairies, gnomes, mermen and mermaids, and all the host of magical beings that cavort in your glens and waters enjoying the beauty of planet Earth.

One key occurrence in this evolutionary step forward will be the ability that humans will develop to see and communicate with these other beings residing on Earth. There will be much rejoicing abroad in the land when this awakening occurs. Laughter, revelry and joy will abound. For these beings supply the playfulness and love that has helped sustain earthlings throughout the dark times of pain and suffering which have been the norm, unfortunately, for those incarnating here.

Ever since the earliest golden ages when all was in harmony and balance, there has been an ever-increasing descent into materiality. This involutionary process where spirit descends deeper into matter is accompanied by ever-growing pain and suffering. This is primarily because of the separation from the true state of all beings — union with the Divine Force.

So it was that a beautiful gift was given earthlings — the presence, albeit unseen, of many others who spread joy, laughter and love to counteract the sorrow that has existed down through every age. We ask that those souls on Earth open themselves to the presence of these other beings and honor their roles in your lives. For those who are able to do this, one day you might just see a laughing, mischievous fairie dancing along with you as you walk in the beauties of your natural world. A primary experience for humans will be reconnecting again with the quality of joy, which is their natural state. The thing that will most accelerate this process is to become aware of all the unseen fairie folk that play, laugh, and love all about you. Can you not feel their presence? Join them. They have been waiting for you for such a long time indeed.

We now would like to turn to conditions on the Earth —climatic, economic, societal and political. Earth changes increased significantly in all of these areas by the middle of 1998. Many are asking, "Are these Earth changes going to occur as predicted?" The answer is yes. Throughout the course of life on the planet there have been periodic shifts and sinking of land masses in order to provide renewal for the planet itself, and also to create a new environment for emerging cultures to experience spiritual growth and development. These changes occur within a long cycle of death and rebirth, which flows through the ethers surrounding this planet. The best way to live within one of the phases of dissolution is to see the longer perspective and join in the excitement at being a part of the human adventure with its corresponding ups and downs. It is an amazing dance, is it not?

The forces of change are gathering and preparing for the Great Shift Forward. It is a time of anticipation for all those entities closely connected to the Earth's unfolding plan. There is excitement and expectation on the part of these spirit entities that have been involved in the ongoing guidance of life on your planet. For many eons, there has been continuous preparation in the dimensions of spirit encircling the Earth. Many beings from throughout the galaxy have come and participated in the unfolding activities, which have been occurring on a continuous basis.

And now the long-awaited time is almost here. There have been many prophecies and descriptions presented throughout the planet as to what this time will be like. All contain a kernel of truth and also much distortion. Those assisting on the level of spirit have knowledge of the basic outlines of the Great Step Forward, but the actual details of the transition are known only at the highest hierarchical levels of the universe.

The following changes are certain. The planet itself will experience great upheavals. Weather conditions in the next ten to fifteen years will become extreme, causing much damage through flood, drought and devastating winds. Basic living conditions, as well as all agricultural activities, will be adversely affected throughout the world. Earthquakes and extensive volcanic upheaval will be the norm.

There will not be a continent that will not feel the effect of this turmoil in the inner Earth. The atmosphere surrounding the planet will be smoky and filled with ash, which will keep out the rays of the sun and cause greater rainfall than normally is produced in any given year. The sea levels will rise, causing destruction along the coastlines of all the continents. The totality of these conditions will cause suffering and dislocation for humans all over the Earth.

In the face of the appearance of these events, each and every country's political and financial support systems will be heavily burdened. Even the wealthiest country in the world, the United States, will be sorely pressed to meet the needs of its citizens. Breakdown of institutions supporting society will occur everywhere. People will suffer from lack of shelter, food and clothing. Governments will crumble because of their inability to provide for those living within their national borders. In summary, the Old World Order is being destroyed so that a New World can be born, fresh with promise for a higher level of living for Earth beings.

So the question immediately arises, "What can one do to prepare for the coming changes described above?" The first decision that has to be made is whether one wants to do anything at all. Every person alive during this period has requested to be here and has a specific idea of what he or she is to do. But the attraction of third-dimensional matter can pull one away from the intent of spirit, resulting in a rejection of that earlier commitment. For each soul has been given the gift of free will by the Great Creator and has the right to exercise it at any given point in time.

For those who wish to ride the wave of this Great Evolutionary Step forward, we have this to say to you. Believe at a deep level of being that these changes are coming. First and foremost, prepare yourselves physically, emotionally, psychologically and spiritually in whatever ways you see best so that you are operating at peak effectiveness when the changes occur. Secondly, learn how to take care of your basic needs for food, clothing, shelter and medicine. Thirdly, attune yourself to spirit and be certain that you are residing in a geographic location that will support you on all levels. Fourthly, insure that there are people living near you who can serve as a support network for you in time of need.

Finally, develop a vision of yourself living at a high level of well being during the times of greatest crisis. Hold this positive vision as you go about preparing yourself on a mundane level for what is to come. Always keep in mind that a new freshness of the land and a rainbow of hope for the future come after a storm of any duration. All of these events will have washed away the Old World and ushered in a new heaven and a new Earth which has been spoken about for many centuries in the past.

Those who are living after The Great Change will serve as pioneers for the coming era. They will rebuild and give birth to new societies all over the Earth within which the children of the Creator will live and laugh and love in the fields of matter. So all of the birth pangs are worth it, are they not?

## The Millennium

Much was written about the year 1998 and its significance in the overall evolutionary scheme. It was described as the beginning of a period of great spiritual, societal and geographic change on planet Earth. And truly it will be seen in this way when those living in the future look back on this time of The Great Step Forward.

In the period from 1993-1998, there was a growing awareness on the part of more and more people that the winds of change were blowing ever stronger throughout the Earth. Weather conditions became more severe and unnatural in many ways. Countries throughout the Earth struggled to maintain a positive political equilibrium in the face of disintegrative forces that seemed bent upon bringing down what appeared to be even the most stable of governments. Modern technology in the highly developed western world was often far ahead of the moral and ethical structures of these societies. There was a level of anxiety among the peoples of many nations as to what the future would hold.

The idea of the Millennium exerted a powerful conceptual overlay on those final years of the twentieth century in the psyches of people living all over the globe. A thoughtform of fear and anticipation took on a life of its own and created its own energy field that exerted an electromagnetic vibration infiltrating all levels of life on Earth. You ask how this could be, that an idea coming to a certain percentage of people could visibly impact humans all over the Earth. When the power of thought is truly understood, it readily will be evident how this could happen.

Mind force contains the greatest power for manifestation in the universe. Nothing at the level of matter can come into existence unless it is first conceived on the plane of mind. This holds true for every dimension of creation throughout time and space. Once this great power is recognized, the act of creation will take on a new and advanced perspective indeed. As more books about the Millennium were written and more people talked and thought about the end of this century, a powerful thoughtform was created surrounding the Earth. It emanated a radioactive frequency infiltrating the very air that people breathe.

It was almost as if the thoughts people were having were returning to them with greater power and intensity. Because these thoughts had not been released with a sense of faith and confidence in the future, they stayed entrapped in the Earth's radioactive forcefield and magnified in strength. Fear and anxiety predominated emotionally, particularly around the idea of the century's end.

A certain segment of people really think that the destruction of the world is near, and many feel that catastrophic change is very possible. When such a large vibratory field of fear and worry impulses the Earth, all areas of planetary functioning are impacted. Even the basic rotational stability of the planet is influenced in an adverse manner.

This entire concept seems beyond belief. But in truth, many

societies down through the ages have understood at a primary level the effect human thoughts and actions have on the health and well being of the planet. That is why many former cultures have held sacred religious rituals to protect and enhance the Earth. Key geographic areas of the Earth were designated as powerful centers requiring stabilization on a continual basis. Certain ancient peoples saw this task as their primary duty and privilege and dedicated themselves to this undertaking.

But down through time, this knowledge has died with the cultures that honored it. The recognition of the Earth as the sustainer of all life has been ignored. Love and responsibility for the planet play no significant role in today's advanced technological societies. That is why the time has come for Earth awareness to be reactivated on all levels. An ecological ethic needs to be reintroduced into the minds and hearts of all human beings living on the planet.

As this process intensifies, people will become aware of the effect actions and thoughts have upon the systems that stabilize and regulate the Earth's functions. Responsible behavior will then become the norm. Balance and harmony will be the order of the day. A brave new world will emerge in the mists of time to come — one where honor and respect for fellow beings and the Earth will be the prevailing ethic that motivates all human interactions.

Now we would like to speak to you regarding the times in which you live. The year of 1998 has long been recognized as a benchmark for the approaching Millennium. Edgar Cayce prophesied that 1958 to 1998 was a period of preparation leading to the end of this current age. It was evident when 1998 ended that a new and very different phase was beginning on planet Earth.

These past forty years have been a time when the destructive energies required to bring about the close of a two thousand-year period have been germinating and starting to coalesce around a spiral vortex of great power. Before a shift of any kind in human affairs can occur, it is necessary that the supportive spiritual forces engendering the change must come together.

This has been the primary function of this period of preparation. Now the changes will start in earnest. First let us speak regarding the physical alterations which will affect the planet in the next fifteen years. Throughout the eons of time in which this planet has existed, it has experienced much evolutionary transformation that was a mirror for the human development occurring on its surface. Since a type of humanoid existence began on Earth millions of years ago, the physical evolution of the planet has marched in step with the human beings it was supporting.

As the recognition of this fact became evident to those incarnating on Earth, rituals and religious practices joined with Earth sciences to ascertain the current condition of the planet and predict in an orderly and accurate fashion what would be transpiring on the surface of the Earth. Certain peoples like the Maya were able to predict with great accuracy what was to come. It was recognized that the Earth needed to purify and cleanse itself on a regular basis to maintain its ongoing vitality and health. And it was known that this cleansing could occur in a wide variety of ways.

What also was known, but not so widely, was the impact that human behavior had upon the weather and the very stability of the core of the planet itself. And so it is that those currently in incarnation find themselves at a most pivotal time indeed. For not only is it the end of a two thousand-year cycle, but also of other larger cycles of time. The concept of time in the universe can best be compared to a giant clock with many different wheels and gears turning in increasingly larger concentric circles. So it is that the end of other greater cycles of time on the planet is drawing near, which creates a powerful energy field for dramatic change.

Physical transformation will occur all over the planet, with some areas being far more impacted than others. A latitudinal band of approximately 20 degrees encircling the Earth in the Northern Hemisphere throughout the temperate zones will be the hardest hit. The primary reason for this is the disharmony and warfare that has existed in the countries occupying these zones all over the Earth. Much destruction will come from earthquakes and volcanic eruptions with severe weather disturbances arising from wind, flooding and drought. If humankind initiates a third world war using nuclear weapons, radioactive radiation will be added to the list of woes with which humans will have to contend.

Along with the disturbances described above, there will be a polar shift of the Earth on its axis. But this shift will be mild compared with others in the far distant past. It will be more of a correction and adjustment in the declination of the angle of the Earth's axis than a great catastrophic reversal. But certain areas of the Earth will be affected, primarily by rising water levels. Some lands will be inundated along the coastlines, and other lands will rise to serve as new, purified regions for human habitation.

Most of these events will occur in the next thirty years, with the vast majority of them ending around 2015. It is wise for those in incarnation on Earth to recognize that they are in for a rough ride in the coming years and to prepare themselves to live these times with as much high well-being as possible.

The most important preparation humans can make is to attune to the Earth and the energy that is radiating all over the globe as these events approach. If they do so, they will know in the depths of their being that what we have said here is true. They will start to use their own inner sensing mechanism, which is their higher spiritual self, to determine what they should do and where they should be at all times, no matter how much their intellect questions this inner knowing. They also must start to feel a sense of joy and anticipation regarding the days ahead. For planet Earth is going through a great rebirth, and those here for it are participating in a cosmic adventure of galactic proportions.

It is most important not to focus on the coming events themselves. For each soul presently incarnating on the Earth has a specific role to play in this cosmic drama and knows at an inner level what that role is.

So follow your internal sensing at all times. Pay no attention to those who would dissuade you from doing what you feel is best. And the operative word here is "feel". For your feelings will serve as your guide in all matters

If a strong sense arises to take a certain course of action, do it. Use your mental, intellectual capabilities to help you determine how to accomplish whatever is needed. But do not allow your intellect to make the decisions and choices. That is not its function, and it will not serve you well if used in that capacity.

The twentieth century was a time of great movements of people all over the globe. Wars, droughts, and Earth disturbances were the catalyst for these migrations; and they will continue to be so. For a reseeding of the planet is in effect. Societal structures and mores are crumbling. And out of the humus of the Old World, a New World is being born. Some people will be responsible for helping the old world die gracefully, while others have a part in establishing new bases with those who will be the pioneers for the coming age. Determine the role you are to play and honor the course that others will take in this divine drama.

And above all, feel a sense of joy and fulfillment for yourself and the world in which you live. For all is in divine order, is it not? At a soul level, you feel peace and tranquillity along with trust for the unfolding of the Divine Plan. That is why it is important to always access that soul wisdom on a daily basis in order to set a smooth course through the rough waters ahead. Know that you are a being of light and love helping to transform the world of matter so that it can truly reflect the divine essence at the core of all that exists.

We now would like to address the societal and cultural changes that will happen in the next fifteen to thirty years. When climatic and Earth disturbances increase, people will turn more and more to their outer world. The time for inner reflection will diminish as people realize more completely that massive changes are occurring all over the globe. There will not be a life on this planet that will not be changed in some significant way.

People will start to think in terms of physical and economic survival rather than the persuit of pleasure. One key question that will arise will be where to live. The great migrations of the twentieth century caused by war, famine and drought will be nothing compared to the movements of people in search of safe lands. There will arise an issue that has previously been of little importance. It is the issue of compatibility. Many will come to realize that part of the safety net needed for the future will be the company of like-minded individuals who share their values.

Recognition will surface that a diversity of talents is essential. Just as the Mormons of America forged a strong group of people who joined together in a common cause, so others will look for a similar situation, only one that is not religiously motivated. The need for compatibility of mind and spirit will grow, particularly within the individuals who agreed before coming into incarnation to serve as pioneers establishing groups to settle in locations which will be prominent for future development. It is important that those moving to new locales, which hold a long-term significance for the unfolding of the Divine Plan, have a basic harmony of values and outlook, even though their age, talents, and backgrounds may be very different.

And so it is that seemingly disparate people from all over the Earth will come together in surprising and synchronistic ways in future years. The inner motivation to relocate in areas far from where they live will come into the consciousness of many individuals who, if told today that this would be, would scoff and turn away in disbelief. But the urges for many will be strong and undeniable. A cross-pollination of people, talents and resources is needed to seed the new age that is coming into existence. The old ways are dying, and so new structures must rise out of the ashes of what was once common practice.

In order for this transformation to occur, well-established societal and national groups all over the globe will crumble and recreate themselves on new foundations. A new way of life will arise on the fertile ashes of the Old World. This is the way it has ever been on planet Earth down through the eons of time. The old age contributes knowledge gained over long periods which becomes a part of the human condition — lessons that do not need to be repeated but which are held as a deep knowing by those who will come after.

And so some of the personal traits that will be essential in the years to come will be openness, receptivity to inner prompting, flexibility, and courage to follow one's convictions. It will be essential to look with joy and understanding at the events unfolding all over the world. Think of the birth process. It is painful and chaotic but totally worth it in all ways. A New World is being born, and those experiencing it are the progenitors for the coming age. What an honor indeed! Step forward with confidence and appreciation for the important role that you are playing, no matter what transpires. All is in divine order and each and every one of you is loved and appreciated.

# Miasms

Those currently living on the Earth are involved in an intense purification of body, mind and spirit. This purification has been projected from the dim reaches of the past into this time in order to facilitate the Great Step Forward which is about to be taken by humanity. Much of the pain and suffering held within the human constitution through the DNA and soul memory must be released. A clear base must be provided for the entrance of the photonic light particles bombarding the Earth in ever larger and more powerful waves.

Every being currently inhabiting the Earth is coping with this release of negativity in whatever way is best for that person. The very etheric web of the Earth is also participating in this great release. All the anger, pain and grief that have been experienced by humans living on this planet are held in a vibratory record encircling the Earth. This record also contains all that has been hopeful, loving and uplifting down through the ages.

The Earth is passing into a part of its galaxy that contains a powerful forcefield of light and radioactivity. In order to absorb these intense waves, the physical body must be strong and centered. The emotions must be clear and steady. And the mind must be open and receptive. Physical miasms held within the body's electromagnetic field need to be released so that the body's energy can be totally directed to the necessary support and maintenance that will be required. The concept of miasms has come forward in recent years through different books and methods of healing. It is imperative that people understand what miasms are and how they affect the human body.

A miasm is an independent energy field existing within the human body, which is not a part of the system of that body. The miasm enters the body during a time of great weakness or vulnerability and becomes a satellite functioning within a larger and separate system. The miasm remains dormant and inactive until the appropriate time arises for the expulsion of this energy field. A person can live a lifetime in which the propitious time for removal of the miasm never arises.

In this case, the miasm is passed down through the genetic pattern of the individual's family as an inherited weakness or propensity for specific physical symptoms that occasionally surface. Since the miasm resides within the physical body's system, it interferes with and draws from the energy field of the body in a subtle but impacting manner.

Miasms are totally self-contained energy vortexes. They exist in a life cycle of their own, which depends upon a parent body for its ultimate energy source. The miasm is created out of a vibratory spiral that comes into existence during a time of intense pain, suffering, grief or confusion. The miasm is literally spun off from the thoughtform creating it and becomes an independent energy entity seeking a host body for its necessary living environment.

Let us describe a scenario in which a miasm is created. A man is fighting in a bitter and long-standing war with invaders to his homeland. He knows that all that he holds dear is at stake — home, family, and country. He can also recognize that the invading army is much stronger and will eventually prevail. And so for days he fights on with increasing dread and fear. His army is pushed back to within a few miles of his village where his wife, family and friends reside. He then recognizes with increased terror that the final great battle will occur in and around his village.

He knows that he and his fellow soldiers cannot prevent the invaders from destroying all that he has known and loved. By this time his emotional body is vibrating at an intense speed with thoughts of anger, fear, grief and despair. He becomes almost manic in his attempts to save and protect his loved ones. Just at that moment, a soldier on horseback attacks him and a few of his comrades who are on foot. His bronze sword is no match for the iron weapon wielded by the enemy. He feels the sword pierce his vital organs in the abdominal area and falls to the ground mortally wounded.

As the life force slowly drains from his body, he can see the invaders enter the town and torch the many small huts where his family and friends live. In his final dying moments, his emotional body emits a powerful vibratory vortex, which condenses into an energy entity called a miasm. It is a forcefield that holds the emotions he was feeling at the time of his death.

This miasm then exists with the single intent of finding a host body, which is open, vulnerable and in a similar emotional state where it can reside. Or the miasm attaches itself to the soul essence of the dying man to be carried into future incarnations as a residual weakness in the abdominal area of future bodies his soul will inhabit.

The DNA is a blueprint of the genetic history of a human being and also contains the history of the soul essence as well. Therefore the miasm becomes part of the hereditary field of the body in which it resides if it is not dispelled during the lifetime in which it was incurred. So it is that many individuals can be impacted down through time by a single event experienced by one person. One of the interesting facets of miasms is that they generally are held in the same area of the body in which the original trauma was located and remain there until a time occurs which will contain all the right elements for removal.

The reason that the topic of miasms is so crucial at this point in time is that miasms block the free flow of energy throughout the body. No matter how strong or healthy an individual is, a miasm is an agent which weakens the human system. A miasmic area contains an energy density that prevents the free flow of the life force in an unimpeded manner. As we have stated earlier, the Earth is moving into an area of the Milky Way Galaxy which contains an increase of photonic particles with higher emissions of light force. The human body needs to develop a different vibratory field that will be receptive to and compatible with these particles.

A body containing a miasm is structurally weakened and will be unable to withstand the coming photonic waves without lapsing into a debilitating illness. Also, at the end of each age, humans need to release and purify their etheric and soul bodies preparatory for new development on the upward turn of the Divine Spiral of Life. And since this is so, the healing of miasms will be of prime importance in the waning years of the Age of Pisces, as it is called on planet Earth.

Clinics will spring into existence that will recognize miasms and offer methods of treatment for removal of these blights to the human body. More and more healers within traditional and alternative medical systems will become aware of the existence of miasms and will develop the treatment required. As people learn that their illness has a spiritual cause and can be treated at the levels of body, mind and spirit, they will take a giant step forward in recognizing the true origin of disease.

The first step needed in combating miasms within the human system is an educational one. That is why sources from the realm of spirit have been bringing this information to the human race all over the globe. Soon the knowledge of the reality of miasms will be widely held by many people throughout the Earth. Then steps will be taken to treat this condition in an effective manner, thereby eradicating a large number of illnesses that have eluded diagnosis down through the years.

So we ask that readers of these words reflect on what we have said here. If you feel that you may possibly have a miasm, find a health professional that will work with you in addressing this condition. Only with direct application and treatment can the science of miasmic release develop.

We would like to comment about the manner in which miasms will be healed. We will speak on a conceptual basis only, since to address this issue specifically would be counter to the plan for the development of miasmic release which will emerge in the coming years as a specific branch of medicine. The time for application of the healing process will occur when the miasm held within a certain area of the body activates into a painful and debilitating condition.

Routine tests will show no physical abnormality that can be diagnosed and treated, because a miasm can only be reflected at the etheric level of the human system. And currently the scrutiny of the body's electromagnetic forcefield is not included in regular diagnostic evaluation. The absence of a concrete diagnosis is the key indicator of the presence of a miasm. In the future, people who are medically intuitive and can see the density that indicates the location of the miasm will be a part of the team identifying the existence of the condition.

Once it has been determined that a miasm is the cause of the illness, a wide variety of treatments will be administered throughout the healing process. If the person is willing and open to the idea of a miasm having been created during another existence, a trained psychologist will guide the individual to the incident where the miasm originated. The person will see and experience the events connected with the onset of the miasm. The act of bringing these events into conscious awareness can shorten and simplify the entire healing process.

The person can then see clearly the cause for the painful condition with which he or she is dealing. It is very hard to convey the power that conscious awareness of the cause of illness brings into the healing process. In the future, this phenomenon will be recognized and utilized on a regular basis by every branch of the healing profession. Only when one recognizes and takes responsibility for the personal role held in the creation of an illness will treatment and healing take a giant step forward.

Once the existence of a miasm is diagnosed and the personal history is identified, a wide range of healing techniques will be used. The electromagnetic forcefield of the body is directly involved in the maintenance of the miasm. And so healing modes will be developed which will impact the body's electrical and nervous systems. The primary purpose here is to loosen the hold of the miasm and start to move it out of the body. The first and foremost step in accomplishing this is providing treatment for the etheric system, which is directly connected to the body's nervous system.

The two most common avenues of treatment for the electrical system used at the present time are flower essences and electric cell application. Neither one is very widely known or used. Edgar Cayce's writings contained the first body of information in current times regarding the electric cell as a method of healing. The great benefit of flower essences was first discovered by Dr. Edward Bach of England and has been added to by people in the United States, especially Machaelle Small Wright. Even though flower essences initially impact the electrical system, their effect then radiates out into the mental and emotional areas of the body in a soothing and healing fashion.

Flower essences will become standard treatment for miasms because of their effectiveness in moving negative emotional states out of the body. It must be remembered that miasms are initially caused by intensely negative emotions that create an independent energy vortex. Therefore, much of the healing of miasms will center on emotional release. Trained therapists will assist in this aspect of healing to the degree that it is advisable. And new, presently unknown, techniques will be discovered which will be directed at the electrical system and emotional body.

The physical environment is another important element in the cure of miasms. The fastest and most effective healing method occurs when the patient is treated in a separate, self-contained setting where all the necessary resources can be provided in a comprehensive manner. There will be treatments for the body that primarily address the physical symptoms alone. A wide variety of healing modes will be manifested, geared specifically to the alleviation of the physical pain the miasm is causing. Many of these modes are currently used for treatment by various disciplines within the healing profession, and others have yet to be discovered.

Each individual will undergo a different amount of therapeutic time with treatment geared to his or her specific case. The importance of miasmic healing will become readily evident on a worldwide scale in the years to come. The positive effect on the levels of human functioning will be seen at a glance. Human beings will become healthier, with higher energy in all areas of their lives. Chronic, undiagnosed, recurring ailments will become a thing of the past. And most important of all, the auric field of humans who have released their miasms, or those who never had them, will be clear and open to receive the new particles of light infiltrating the electromagnetic field of the Earth.

These vibratory waves are the catalyst for the Great Step Forward which humanity is about to take on planet Earth. We have spoken at some length before about this evolutionary step for which humans have long prepared. It is a time much anticipated by indigenous cultures around the globe. Their task, which was to keep the world in harmony and balance with sacred rituals until the Great Step Forward occurs, will be ended. Their work will cease, and they will pass from the Earth. We all need to honor and salute them for a job well done. Without them the new heaven and new Earth that is dawning would never have been possible. Many thanks, dear friends, for the centuries of service you have performed on behalf of the Divine Plan.

# Earth's Healing Crisis

In the times of turbulence that are fast approaching, it will be imperative that those moving through the increased vibrational waves know how to adapt and recharge their bodies in order to maintain a state of high well-being. In the course of the next twenty years, the Earth itself will experience a comprehensive catharsis. Since the Earth possesses a spiritual essence just like all other conscious beings, its healing crisis will resemble that of a human being in the throes of recovery from a longtime, serious illness. For that is exactly what the Earth has been experiencing for millennia.

As humans have been moving through the densest time on the Earth since its creation, the Earth has been most adversely affected indeed. Humans, by and large, have forgotten their deep and ongoing connection to the great being that sustains their lives. They no longer view the Earth as their mother at a deeper level of planetary support and sustenance. And because of this separation, they have misused and abused the Earth in a deeply harmful manner. Only the indigenous people in isolated pockets all over the planet have kept this ancient knowing with its accompanying practices alive.

The beings on this planet are participating in a great awakening. It can best be described as it was in the fairy tale of the sleeping beauty. She slept for a long period before her prince awakened her with a kiss of love. There is a close parallel here to what is occurring on the Earth at this time. The irradiating subatomic particles that are beginning to appear in the Earth's forcefield have the primary essence of Love. Great work has been performed here in this far-off corner of the galaxy by souls dedicated to the furtherance of the Universal Divine Plan. It is now time for the loving harvest to begin. The new millennium will be the beautiful expression of that harvest as it touches all aspects of life on Earth.

But in order for this era of peace and connection to All That Is to begin, the final sweeping away of all the negativity of the past must be completed. The last one hundred years of the twentieth century carried the assignment of this great cleansing. The old ways have served their purpose and must be removed from the stage to create space for the next act to begin. What an amazing period it has been! What great strength and commitment it has taken to stay the course during the densest time of separation and materialism that has ever existed on the Earth! What a great drama of the Divine has unfolded!

Can you learn to revel in this time and let go of the suffering and trauma it has contained? It has been an amazing ride, has it not? But it is time to move on. There is a whole new act emerging in this divine drama. Welcome the dissolution and destruction that is necessary to pave the way for the coming age with its more highly developed species of humans that will inhabit the Earth.

Those that are currently in incarnation are the progenitors of the new root race. The extrasensory skill and abilities that some are developing will be the norm for the people of the future. Therefore it is imperative for those who hold this role to embrace the capabilities they are learning. Never view yourself as weird or apologize for the multidimensional capacities that you are evidencing. You agreed before coming on the Earth plane for this life that you would assume this responsibility at a certain prescribed point in time. So embrace the experience of growing into a being of greatly expanded sensory awareness. It will be akin to surfing a giant wave that carries you over the waters of life with the exhilaration of a great task well done!

## September 11 – A Day of Karmic Cleansing

It is now time for us to look at the events of September 11, 2001 so we can see the significance of what happened here from a broader, spiritual perspective. It is apparent to most that the attack on the two towers of the World Trade Center in New York City was an event of momentous significance. In fact, many have been heard to say that their world has been changed in a profound and irreversible way.

This insight is accurate. Life on your planet will never go back to the way it was before September 11. And that is a blessing. An expanded world of great beauty is waiting to be born out of the agony of your times. And so it is that we ask Americans, particularly, to see with clarity and comprehension the true significance of this painful day.

For these events will be remembered far into the future as the seminal incidents ushering in the beginning of a new age for humankind. Every culture has a date around which its consciousness forms group identification and remembrance. September 11 is the date serving as this dividing line between the old times and the new.

So we ask you look with an open mind and heart as we describe the spiritual energies that were in force on that memorable day in the affairs of those living on the Earth. We have already spoken with you regarding the triangulation of energies that must be in effect for a creative endeavor to manifest. And so it was that three spiritual energies were acting as the power of transformation for your dying world. They were psychic release, divine reckoning, and atonement.

These three pillars of spiritual power were operating on that day and had assisted earlier in bringing the events of September 11 to fruition. We ask that you walk with us to look more closely at the forces that were in the ascendancy during these hours of power.

## Psychic Release

As people all over the world watched in horror on the morning of September 11, three American planes hit the two World Trade towers and the Pentagon, causing extensive death and destruction. Because of the advances in communication technology that have occurred in the last fifty years, thousands were able to observe the events as they happened or soon afterwards. The significance of the simultaneous reaction of horror, grief and disbelief from so many cannot be underestimated.

Those of us on the realm of spirit were able to observe a thought-form of powerful negative intensity envelop the Earth within a very short period. The astral plane surrounding the Earth holds the psychic, emotional energy felt by all those living on your planet. This band of psychic energy took on the characteristics of a dense and penetrating fog that ebbed and flowed in the locales where there was the highest emotional reaction to these events.

Obviously, the United States was affected the most severely, but so were many other areas, as an emotional wave of tremendous power spread rapidly over the Earth. The Muslim world was highly agitated, as it became evident that individuals from their nations were implicated. They knew they would be held accountable and great suffering would ensue as a result.

Yes, there were some that praised the death and destruction as evidence of God's punishment. But the Creator of all That Is upholds the principles of Life and Love. Death and destruction are the fruits of humanity's fall into ignorance and separation from God's grace. Down through the history of human beings on Earth, there have many examples of holy wars supposedly fought in God's name. This could never be so, since the light of the Creator can never shine in the darkness of war.

The psychic release of intense emotion that occurred on September 11 extended far beyond the events of this day and people's reaction to them. Since this was a global experience, its sheer magnitude and power ripped open the psychic thoughtform encircling the Earth that contains all the ancient emotional energies, which have been waiting centuries for release.

Those presently living on the Earth plane are participating in the ending of a series of time cycles, the longest of which is 500,000 years. It is now necessary to clean out and remove negative psychic energy so that a new cycle can begin from a fresh position of strength and power. This is why the events of September 11, as destructive and painful as they were, had a deeper spiritual purpose that ultimately would bring about a higher good for everyone.

All of the emotional energy of pain, anguish, suffering, fear and destruction that was held on the astral plane around the Earth now has been released. For a time there will be great turbulence for those living on the planet. Weather conditions will become more chaotic and unpredictable. Powerful storms, earthquakes, tornadoes and drought will become the norm as the Earth struggles to regain equilibrium while she is buffeted by the intense energy that has been liberated.

The very hounds of hell have been freed as war, conflict and strife become more widespread all over the Earth. Even the most centered and stable people will be hard pressed to keep their balance during the coming years. It seems to be a most negative message indeed that we bring to you. But from a spiritual point of view, all is in divine order.

What we ask of you, our beloved friends on the Earth plane, is to view these times from the perspective of spirit. What you are experiencing now is a global housecleaning of negative emotional energy. Think how wonderful it feels when you clean out any area of your house that has been filled with old and unused items cluttering your living space. Transpose this picture of a personal housecleaning to one of a necessary global cleansing. Then you will be able to experience what is happening with a peaceful and calm acceptance, trusting that all is well, even though on the surface it appears to be just the opposite.

In order to maintain this state of acceptance, it will be necessary to develop daily practices of prayer and meditation. There are many individual and group souls working with higher spiritual powers to give you support. The Christ Consciousness is beaming continuous Light and Love to your planet. At a certain point, all the efforts on the human and spiritual realms will coalesce into a great shift of consciousness ushering in a new and more highly evolved age for all. So gird yourselves.

Strengthen yourselves physically, emotionally, psychologically and spiritually. You are all midwifing the birth of a New World!

Divine Reckoning

The second force operating on September 11 to bring about the transformation of your world was divine reckoning. Let us be clear about what the term "reckoning" really means here. It refers to a settling of long overdue penalties for past actions. In the universes of the Creator, there is a Law of Cause and Effect that has been in operation since the beginning of time. It is the ultimate spiritual system of justice. It has been called karma by many on the Earth plane.

You might wonder what past actions by the United States required a penalty resulting in such extensive pain and suffering"? Quietly reflect for a moment on the events of this century. We ask you to look at the decision the United States made at the end of World War II to drop an atomic bomb on the Japanese cities of Nagasaki and Hiroshima. The choice made by the American military and political leaders activated the cosmic Law of Cause and Effect the moment it was carried out.

In order for justice to prevail in your universe, it was necessary that the karmic scales be balanced. And so the Law of Cause and Effect was activated symbolically to the letter. The two Japanese cities were destroyed and thousands were killed. In retribution, the two towers of the World Trade Center were destroyed and thousands of people in New York City also died. Is it not readily apparent how this divine law manifests?

Since the American military carried out the political directive, its headquarters in the Pentagon were also a target for karmic balancing. It is significant, however, that only one portion of the building was destroyed. Divine penalties are always directly in proportion to the payment required. In World War II, the American military led the battle for freedom against the Axis powers that attempted to enslave the world. So the American military command center was damaged but not destroyed. The account was settled in full.

There is a profound significance in the fact that American planes hit the World Trade Towers and the Pentagon, even though non-Americans overpowered the crews and forced the actions that followed. Again, the Law of Cause and Effect came into play. The atomic bombs that leveled the two Japanese cities were dropped from an American airplane. And in the events of September 11, American airplanes again became the instruments of divine justice.

We know these words will be upsetting to many that read them. You will say that the bombings of the Japanese cities were a necessary act of war. We would ask that you attend to our view of war. It may help you see the deeper underlying spiritual theme that runs through this entire question. Violence against any person, group or country is never acceptable in the eyes of God. The highest prevailing energy in all the Creator's universes is Love; and since war is the opposite of Love, it can never be upheld.

You may ask, "What if you or your family or country is attacked, can you not defend yourselves"? Our answer is yes, but only with the absolute minimum of force and no more. Always the least destructive and least hurtful course must be taken. That is the way of Love. As more information becomes available about the decision to drop the atomic bombs, it will be seen that those actions exceeded the spiritual standard of the least destructive and least hurtful course.

We are not suggesting that those who have perpetrated acts of death and destruction should not be held accountable for their actions. We would remind you that the Law of Cause and Effect has been activated against all of the individuals who planned and carried out the events of September 11, even though they served as instruments of divine justice.

You may ask, "Will this chain of cause and effect ever end?" This is a most important question indeed. Our answer to you is that when every soul on the Earth plane can act in a state of unconditional love and peace towards self and others, the spiritual Law of Cause and Effect will cease to exist. Then, and only then, will there be a new Heaven and a new Earth.

## Atonement

It is now time to speak about the third force at work on September 11 – that of atonement. We will address two levels of atonement, earthly and spiritual. In your world, atonement generally means making amends for wrongdoing. As explained above, the bombing of the World Trade Towers and the Pentagon were the payment exacted for the United States' actions in World War II against the Japanese.

But there is a greater debt due for actions taken by the United States that are secret and unknown to the public at large. Certain prominent Americans in concert with other powerful international figures have orchestrated destructive happenings in pursuit of economic and political domination worldwide. This fact has been well hidden from the general public, both in America and other countries throughout the globe.

But the Law of Cause and Effect grinds on inexorably. Accounts of the activities of these individuals are starting to surface, slowly but surely, like water breaking through a dam. The uncovering of the truth will continue to intensify until the magnitude of the unholy conspiracy is brought forth for all to see. As information regarding the deeds of this cabal is assimilated by people all over the Earth, an outcry will ensue that will reach the very heavens themselves.

The grasp of power and control held by these conspirators must be broken, in order to open the gates and let in the light of dawn. Then, and only then, can the people of Earth move on into the new age waiting in the wings. How will this end be accomplished? We would like to address this important question with you in depth.

The people of Earth, Americans especially, need to develop a stance of detached scrutiny. They need to realize that they are being manipulated by a massive cover-up and misinformation effort. They need to increase their powers of discrimination and intuition to sense whether the accounts they are being given by the media and key political figures are truthful or not. This is a finely honed human ability, which will be the norm for the new species that is starting to arrive on the Earth plane.

Those who care about the course of world events must become knowledgeable and informed. Ignorance is a fertile breeding ground for powers that want to control. The greatest support for democracy is an informed populace that insists freedom be upheld at all costs. Knowledge, discrimination and the willingness to act are the human capabilities needed in this situation.

But you may wonder how this topic relates to September 11. There is a direct relationship. The events of September 11 were a balancing of divine justice, but they also were connected to a wider scheme of international control and domination. Atonement will be required of all of those individuals who are perpetrating this effort. And their downfall, when it happens, will be brought about by the American people themselves demanding that their country return to the principles for which it was founded. Many others worldwide will follow suit, causing a shift in the Earth's critical energy mass, which will raise consciousness to a higher level.

The events of September 11 initiated a series of acts that will require reparation and expiation by the perpetrators at all levels. The process of divine justice will unfold in the days, months and years ahead — of this you can be sure. Again, deeper symbolism comes into play. Just as American planes were the instruments of divine justice, so will the American people be a catalyst for the destruction of those who want to dominate and control.

Now, let us turn to atonement as it manifests on the level of spirit. Here it operates in an entirely different manner. It is not exacting satisfaction for wrongdoing or injury, as on Earth. Instead it involves the process of attunement to the Love Principle of the Creator. In order for a soul to achieve this state, at-one-ment with the God Force must be reached.

When at-one-ment is achieved, the soul is filled with an overwhelming love and connection to all of creation. It is simply not possible to hurt anything in any way. Reparations and amends are unnecessary, because one has reached a state where no harm will be given. As you can see, at-one-ment on the plane of spirit is very different than atonement on the level of matter.

At-one-ment is actively at work in the aftermath of the events of September 11. Because of the extent and severity of humanity's destructive actions, the higher powers on the spiritual plane are activating the Law of At-one-ment as the remedy needed to bring the Earth back into balance. At-one-ment is being beamed to Earth from many sources within your universe to join with the mundane level of atonement operating here.

This brings us to speak about the many souls who ended their earthly existence on September 11. The pain and suffering felt by their loved ones is contributing to the emotional psychic release the Earth is experiencing at the present time. In no way do we want to diminish or minimize the personal agony of losing a loved one in such a violent manner. It is one of the deepest of human pains. We hope, however, our following words will help somewhat to assuage the suffering and loss of those remaining.

Every soul coming into incarnation agrees to a specific purpose for the current lifetime. Those who were killed consented, before coming into human form, to contribute their own lives on behalf of a higher purpose. It may be difficult for those left behind to accept this idea, but everyone who was killed on that fateful day understood it at the deeper soul level.

When so many souls ascended simultaneously, there were countless beings helping them in their transition and praising them for their commitment to the unfolding of the Divine Plan. Soon they were able to understand what their soul's commitment had been. They began to feel a deep sense of satisfaction. They knew that they had assisted the human race in attuning to its Divine Source. So love them, praise them, remember them and let them go. They carried out with valor what they came here to do. They deserve all our love and honor for the service they have performed.

# The World to Come

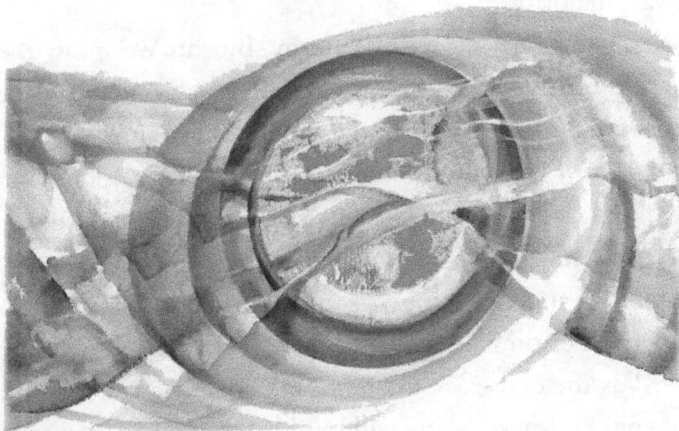

We would like to speak to those of you reading these words regarding the future. We want to relay to you some of the upcoming events that are going to be a significant part of your lives, as well as the lives of all those living on planet Earth during the next twenty years. As Earth moves more fully into the influence of the band of photonic particles that are emanating from Alcyone, the spiritual center of your universe, momentous events will be occurring on all levels.

Tremendous transformation is in the offing. This change will occur physically, emotionally, psychologically, and spiritually. A great cycle of many eons is coming to an end, with dissolution and destruction being the means by which this will be accomplished. In the immediate time ahead, there will grow a faint recognition that a new order is emerging on Earth and that these are the necessary birth pains needed to initiate the process.

A great turn of the evolutionary spiral is about to begin. Human beings on the planet are being illuminated with galactic impulses that will change their genetic structure and reactivate their DNA helixes so that they will be able to function at a much higher level than has previously been possible. Over a given period of time in the future, abilities which have been known to only a very few will become common performance for the vast majority.

Clear-sightedness will be the norm. By this we mean the ability to see auras, energy fields, events appearing afar, and all manner of spiritual unfolding at higher dimensional levels. Humans will be able to see and know behavior at an energetic level. Lies and distortions of truth will no longer be possible since people will know the essence of each matter intuitively.

Physically, humans will be stronger and healthier and will live for longer periods of time not believed possible in this age. Death will not be viewed as the end of all existence but merely a transition to a new form of consciousness. Many will be able to retain their current bodies by constantly rejuvenating them. They then will be able to reassemble them at different dimensional levels by restructuring their subatomic particles to merge with the vibratory matrix of the new location. So the concept of death, as it is currently held, will be considered a primitive belief not clearly understood.

Humans will be able to master the gravitational force field of this planet and easily perform what would be considered astounding feats, such as levitation, walking on water, bilocation, and invisibility, to name a very few. Human bodies will become finer and less dense in molecular structure, emitting a much greater degree of light. As the human vibrational frequency increases through activation by the photonic particles, a different physical form will emerge. It will be a body of great beauty and grace with what would now seem as superhuman powers.

Humans of the future will have strong and steady emotional and psychological natures. Many of the dynamics of control, manipulation, anger, self-centeredness and greed will be viewed as abhorrent behavior characteristics requiring immediate therapeutic attention. There will exist everywhere clinics and healing centers, whose primary function will be to cleanse, purify and realign the electromagnetic forcefield of the body to bring it from a state of disharmony into balance.

The degenerative diseases of today will be things of the past. It will be recognized that all illness stems from separation from the spiritual core of the being. The primary healing mode will be that of realignment with the higher self. Once an individual exhibits behavior that is recognized as disharmonious, he or she will promptly access treatment from a healing center in order to reestablish balance. The individual will know at a soul level that treatment is needed and will voluntarily seek it out.

# Love of Self

We would like to speak further with you regarding the changes that have been occurring at the end of the Age of Pisces. This title identifies the past two thousand years in the minds of many, which is why we use it here. During this time, there was great emphasis on the blood family, the relationship between parent and child, and the interaction between the individual and the larger institutions in society.

Every soul incarnating on Earth during this time experienced lives where these issues were paramount. The astrological designations are just terms used to identify the human archetypal eras of time where certain lessons of learning were the norm. And so it is that for the past two thousand years, humans have struggled, grown and acquired knowledge of basic truths while living under conditions that brought them forth. One of the greatest crucibles for growth has been within parent-child and family relationships.

From the dim reaches of time past, a strong societal value emerged around the importance and dominance of the parental role. This value emphasized that honor, respect and obedience were to be accorded parents at all times, whether warranted or not. The Mosaic Law included the injunction to "honor thy father and mother" as one of its key commandments. All cultures placed a high value on the role of authority — familial, religious or governmental. One of society's main functions was to uphold authority figures at all costs, which was considered key to ongoing stability and security.

Only rarely was the authority figure or group held responsible for the manner in which they treated others. The total societal emphasis rested solely on the duty and obligation of those who were interacting with authority figures, and not the other way around. People who offered resistance or revolted against those in positions of authority, whether personal or public, were considered dangerous and in need of strong disciplinary action, even unto death. Rebellion against authority struck fear into the hearts of family members as well as others in the culture, since it attacked the very cornerstone upon which the society was founded.

All those living on planet Earth are moving into a different time with new lessons and spiritual themes. The single most important step now in the spiritual journey of humankind is to connect and merge with one's own individual essence. It is time to honor, respect and love the self on its journey back to reunion with the God Force. One cannot honor, respect and love the self when one allows oneself to be dominated, controlled or mistreated by anyone in a position of authority.

And so it is that the old dispensation of "honor thy father and mother" no longer will be upheld as necessary under all conditions. There are parents who are unloving, cruel and abusive and therefore undeserving of honor under any circumstances. In fact, to do so is to not honor and love self, which will be one of the highest commandments of this new age.

The most important teaching of the next two thousand years will be to love self. In the broadest sense, knowing and loving self will bring an awareness that we are all one with the Creator and everything that exists in the many universes of time and space. Everyone must learn that there is no separation from one's self, from one's God, from any other living being or from those on the plane of spirit.

The new age will be a time of great unity and coming together. In order to reach this level of existence it will be necessary to elevate the principles of Love and Truth. Those living in the Piscean Age have focused on the teaching of loving one's fellow man while paradoxically perpetrating some of the cruelest inhumanities that have ever been experienced on this Earth. Jesus the Christ spoke to the love of self when he taught all to love the Lord their God with their whole heart and soul, and to love their neighbor as themselves. This love of self that Jesus spoke to did not evolve during these past two thousand years.

It is now time for humankind to take the next major evolutionary step forward — that of being reunited with its own spiritual center. It will be important for every soul to honor self above all, because self is God. When this is accomplished, the love and respect for one's fellow human beings, as well as for all of life, will follow as surely as day follows night.

And so the old dispensation needs to be set aside to be replaced by the new law — Love of Self. There will be those that will not be able to make this transition. They will become the resistors of the new age. You see them marshalling their forces worldwide at the present time. Many of society's values and customs will be shattered all over the Earth in the coming years. But humanity will emerge from the wreckage differently constituted on a new foundation, which will be more in harmony with the values of the next age.

Instead of duty and obligation being required where it is not deserved, love and respect will be the underlying value supporting all human interactions. Responsibility will first be to self and then to those to whom one has given a commitment for love and/or support. Any relationship containing pain or hurt will be deemed undesirable to the high well being of the individuals involved and respectfully will be ended.

Throughout the Earth, cultures will form that are will be dedicated to the uplifting of all of life, or they will not be able to sustain themselves. This is what Jesus the Christ meant when he told his followers that there would come a new heaven and a new Earth.

# A Time of Transformation

Most human beings on planet Earth have been cut off from their spiritual source for a long period of time. As the Middle Ages ended and the western world moved into a period of emphasis on reason, science and intellectual learning, the doors between the many dimensions of spirit and matter closed ever so slowly. Earthlings found themselves cut off from their source of spiritual sustenance. The growing dependency upon the intellectual ego self to chart the course for life became the norm. This phase in humankind's development was programmed into the scenario created for life on planet Earth and is truly perfect in all ways.

In order for the great evolutionary step forward to be realized at its highest level, it was necessary that a strong, recognizable contrast to be in existence when the Great Shift occurs. This planet is moving into a time when it will make a step forward of major proportions. At the physical level this change will manifest as an increase in light particles which will infiltrate all aspects of life, both animate and inanimate, on the Earth. These subatomic particles will change the physical environment dramatically.

New species of flora and fauna will appear to beautify and nourish those souls who will be incarnating here in the future. The waters throughout the Earth will be irradiated with a vibratory energy field that will purify and renew them at all levels. There will come a time when there truly will emerge a new heaven on Earth.

Great changes also will occur in the emotional and psychological natures of those beings inhabiting the Earth. The powerful negative forcefield of fear, anger, and grief with all of its supporting thought forms will disappear from the vibratory matrix of the Earth. It will be recognized how destructive these emotions are at a basic level of being. People will operate more and more from a basis of love and respect for all.

The reason for this is that the basic component of light contains the element of love in its most powerful form. Whenever more light enters any place or situation, there will be evidence of increased harmony and balance. Where one finds harmony and balance, the love of Prime Creator is manifesting at a high level. The primary essence of the Godhead of this universe is love. This divine quality permeates the fabric of life in its varied forms, constantly sustaining and renewing all that exists.

The greatest transformation that will occur will be in the area of communication between the planes of spirit and matter. The concept of two differing realms totally opposite in essence will disappear. It will be as if spirit and matter have fused and are operating as one. The higher centers of the brain will be open to the many dimensions of spirit, receiving and sending in a continual pattern of interaction. The species of human that will evolve after the Great Step forward will be typified by the light, love and beauty radiating from their activated spiritual core. They will experience bliss as a natural and ongoing state — one that has been their birthright from the beginning.

So we speak to all those who will read these words: Remember what we say here. It is your promise for the future, never to be forgotten as you participate in the birth pangs, which are causing such pain and suffering at this time on the Earth. Just as a beautiful child is born after the pain of birth, so are a new heaven and a new Earth waiting in the wings to manifest. And all those living on the Earth now are truly precursors ushering in this new age of light, love and beauty. Never forget this fact. Lift your heads and your hearts. Those who occupy the Earth in the future will remember all that you have done with great gratitude.

# Universal Frequency Band

At this time on the Earth very few individuals are in direct contact with the realm of spirit for the purpose of receiving information and guidance. There is very little recognition that there are many dimensions of spirit which interact and imprint the realms of matter in a direct and concrete way. In fact, everything that exists in matter has first been conceived and brought into being at the level of spirit. Every idea and every act originates in an electromagnetic vibrational forcefield unseen and generally unknown to those living on the Earth plane.

In the past three hundred years, western cultures have been immersed in an era when rational, logical thought and reason were held as desirable standards for human interaction. This focus brought about a complete emphasis upon the material aspects of life. The human ego became the director of personal thought and action, and all contact with the intuitive and spiritual element of one's nature atrophied for the vast majority of people in incarnation during these times.

The left hemisphere of the brain was glorified and continually used down through the years in all areas of life. Therefore a severe imbalance grew in the affairs impacting human life. The deeply ingrained knowledge that all beings living on Earth are endowed with abilities that constitute a birthright of the spirit was slowly forgotten. People turned to science and reason as the guiding force in their lives. The legacy of thousands of years of spiritual knowledge and practice which had been in existence on the Earth were set aside for what was considered a new and better way.

And so it was that the societies on the Earth followed a materially oriented approach to life as they developed more and more sophisticated technology. And thus they became increasingly unbalanced in every area of their lives. Harmony, beauty and attunement to the Earth and all of its creatures, which were held in high value by earlier societies, were discarded as prevailing mores and were replaced by an intense desire to grow and conquer the Earth in every way possible. The daily spiritual rituals and practices once widely followed were discontinued and forgotten over time.

But it must be remembered that everything that occurs on the Earth is part of a great evolutionary plan set into motion by the Creative Forces at the outset of this period of manifestation. The purpose of life here on the Earth plane is to spiritualize matter. This statement is so simple and yet so profound that it bears repeating. The purpose of life here on the Earth plane is to spiritualize matter. And since this is so, the forces of matter must be at their strongest in order to hold the enlightening process when it accelerates. This is why a period of intense development of the concrete mind, with its emphasis on the material, had to take place in preparation for what lay ahead.

The process by which matter is spiritualized is simply one of enlightenment. Light particles of ever-increasing power will come into the forcefield of the Earth, infiltrating all that lives on the planet. In the coming fifteen years, the enlightenment of the Earth will reach a level of intensity never experienced before. Photonic light particles will be increasing in magnitude and impact. They will bring about a change and mutation in the molecular structure of the bodies and minds of the human beings living on the planet. People will become light infused at such a level that their very bodies will become less dense and more spiritualized.

As this process of spiritualization magnifies, those who are able to handle the increased vibrations will find themselves changed at a basic and fundamental level. Their powers of mind, both concrete and abstract, will grow greater. Their psychic and intuitive capabilities will expand as they learn to attune more readily to the realm of spirit. They will know through actual experience that the many levels of spirit exist, and they will be able to access them directly and personally.

One of the greatest discoveries to come will be that of the universal frequency band of information, which has existed down through the eons of time. This band wafts and undulates through the ethers of space and time like a ribbon of shimmering light. It contains all the knowledge and information that could ever be needed on any subject. The Internet of the computers of today is a faint replica of this spiritual phenomenon.

Earth beings will come to know that they have readily available to them at any time a vast reservoir of information on any topic that they may need or want. They no longer will have to speculate or live in the darkness of ignorance. They will learn to quiet themselves, focus on the frequency band, formulate with strong intent the information they wish to receive and it will come into their minds easily and completely.

As attunement to the universal frequency becomes widespread, life on the planet will take an evolutionary step forward of great magnitude. Humans will become enlightened beings, a part of the universal community. They will know that they live on a planet within a galaxy, which is teeming with life of all types and varieties. They will grow to participate in this life stream ending forever the years of darkness and isolation that have existed for so long. They will become partners in the Divine Plan of the Creator that is to include the participation of all of life in a beautiful symphony of cosmic proportions. It has been well worth the waiting and the work involved, has it not?

# The Great Cleansing

It is now necessary to remove any blocks or darkness in your auric fields that will inhibit the ability to operate out of your own personal power at any given point in time. Bringing the light of true awareness to who you are and what you have experienced in this lifetime is an essential ingredient in reclaiming that power. What one is doing to personally become clear in all ways physically, emotionally, mentally and spiritually is akin to what is happening on a planetary level to the Earth and all of its inhabitants.

This is the time of the Great Cleansing, long awaited by the indigenous peoples all over the world. We have spoken before regarding this cleansing but would like to continue on with more information about this matter. For, cleansing the buildup and residue from the past occurs on a regular and predictable basis down through the ages.

What makes this current cleansing of a greater magnitude is its point in time. At least three cycles, each of successively greater length, are coming to a close. The Maya with their sophisticated system of counting time would be able to identify immediately the major significance of this period on Earth. We ask that you trust the import of what we say here, without a detailed description of the cycles themselves. Whenever anything of magnitude comes to a conclusion, there is a period of clearing away the debris and refuse remaining from the activity of the effort. It is ever thus.

This is particularly so when cycles of time in any society comes to an end. Usually throughout the duration of any period, a crystallization of thoughts, ideas, practices and customs gradually develops. The longer these exist in a culture, the more entrenched they become. And so the Plan of the Divine Creator always provides a time for dissolution of all that is finished and no longer needed, in order that the new cycle may begin. The time of clearing and cleansing is an integral part of the ongoing development of both the worlds of spirit and matter. It is essential that one understands this concept and is able to recognize how it is working in this day and age.

And so all that has been the traditional way will end. Values that have upheld societies will change, bringing about an emergence of new and differing mores and beliefs. Customs that have been in effect for long periods will be dropped as people embrace a New World — one, which has been long-awaited on planet Earth. To those who rely on a secure and stable base that is safe and reliable, the days and years ahead will be painful indeed. For there will be no anchor to which anyone can cling; all will be in a state of flux.

Currently there is much speculation regarding the times ahead. The recognition has grown slowly over the past twenty years that a new age is dawning and that a shift of monumental proportions is taking place in all areas of life for those beings living on the Earth. A thousand-year time frame has come to an end, with many referring to the next thousand years as the Millennium.

Throughout this book we have given much attention to describing the new species that will inhabit the Earth in the future. We have defined in detail the capabilities these great beings will have. And we have acknowledged the importance of the role that those presently residing on the planet have played as pioneers. Now we would like to speak about the Earth herself and the changes that will occur in the near future for this great being.

For the Earth is a conscious entity of magnitude and power. Everything that exists in the universe has an indwelling spirit, no matter how large or small, animate or inanimate. So it is that every planet, star and sun is imbued with a spiritual awareness and connection to the Creator and is a part of the unfolding of the Divine Plan. The knowledge of what we have said here will bring Earth beings into a higher dimensional awareness of who they truly are and why they are living on the planet at the present time.

Just as those in physical form undergo major transformations at key junctures in their lives, the Earth also sustains major transfigurations in her essence and makeup. These changes are initiated at the level of spirit and are reflected in the electromagnetic forcefield surrounding the planet. They then appear as physical realignments and new placements of land formations all over the globe, providing a clear picture of the inner transformation that the Earth is experiencing on the spiritual level.

So a question immediately arises regarding the coming Earth changes, which have long been predicted. Given what we have said here, what is the Earth experiencing now, and how will it affect the present areas of land and water? First, we would like to address the question regarding the process of the Earth's spiritual transformation. For the coming realignment of land all over the planet will only be a reflection of the deep inner change going on for her at all levels.

In order for the beings residing on this planet to increase in their abilities, physically, emotionally, mentally and spiritually, the environment needs to be in harmony with their vibrational makeup. Therefore the Earth is raising the vibratory level of her essence just as the human beings living on her surface are doing. The process of transformation is similar to the change that occurs in alchemy where a substance is transmuted to a higher physical form. The energy bringing about this transformation is that of fire, which burns away the dross of the lower elements and creates something of finer composition and character.

So, as the Earth embarks upon this initiation to a higher vibratory level, the fires of her death and subsequent rebirth are manifested physically in increased earthquake and volcanic activity. These fire-activated destructive forces of nature accomplish at the level of matter what Mother Earth is experiencing on the level of spirit. She is presently moving through a major period of expansion that is disruptive and painful. She is actually feeling what could be described as the death throes of a human being, with the same physical agony, grief and despair that people feel when they or their loved ones die.

However, her expanded spiritual awareness gives her the knowledge and wisdom to see what is currently happening to her in a larger perspective. She knows that all is in divine order and for the highest good. So she surrenders herself to the fires of transformation with enduring self-sacrifice. For she understands that the human beings living within her energy field must grow and progress. In order for them to do so, she has to provide a new and expanded electromagnetic energy field which will be compatible and nurturing and will enhance The Great Step forward the human species is about to take.

We ask that all those reading these words reflect upon them in the silence and gather them to your heart. Can you feel somewhere deep within your essence the caring that this great being, the Earth, has for you and all that lives within her vibrational field? In the future, those living on the Earth will be closely attuned to her and will live in a way that is loving and respectful to her as the primary source of their physical survival.

The greatest service you can offer your Mother Earth is to live in harmony and balance. Nurture and respect her, always acting in a manner that promotes peace and goodness for those about you. By so doing, you will help usher in the new heaven and new Earth that has long been awaited down through the eons of time.

Can you not feel the influx of joy and love which is changing your world and all that resides in it? Even though it may not be outwardly apparent, a tremendous influx of uplifting spiritual vibrations is infiltrating and transforming everything about you, hour by hour and day by day. Open yourself up to them. Then you will join the Earth and share with her in the great process of spiritual expansion she is undertaking.

Now as to the second part of the question we asked above. We would like to speak about how the Earth's transformation will affect the present areas of land and water located all over the planet. In an earlier section we supplied information about the adjustment of the Earth's axis and the corresponding impact it will have upon the world's coastlines. We assured you that this correction would be gentler than those in the past have been.

However, we do not want to be misleading in any way concerning future land changes. For at the end of the next two hundred years, the configurations of the continents will be far different than they are today. The spiritual growth and expansion of Mother Earth will be reflected physically in a splitting open along weakened tectonic plate lines and in other vulnerable earthquake areas throughout the globe.

The axial tilt, coupled with extensive volcanic and earthquake activity, will bring much stress upon the existing landmasses. This process will extend slowly over the period of two centuries, with many existing portions of land sinking below the oceans, while other areas will be raised, supplying dry land for new habitation. After this period of realignment, the maps of the world will show a far different picture than that of today.

For an extended time, many areas of the Earth will reflect the inner turmoil that the planet is experiencing. High winds, flooding and increased rainfall caused by atmospheric turbulence will be the norm. People will have to learn to attune to the forces of nature for their very sustenance and survival. Where and how to live will be the key question in the minds of all. The migrations of the twentieth century have been a minor precursor compared to those that will occur in the next two hundred years.

On every existing continent, there will be select areas that will be much less affected, providing havens for settlement. We know that books have been printed recently speaking to this issue and giving information regarding lands that will be safe. We honor these works since they are alerting many to what will come. However, we will not supply specific information covering key lands of safety for the future.

There are two reasons we choose not to do so. First, we cannot emphasize strongly enough that the future physical changes on the planet will be merely a reflection of the spiritual transformation that the Earth will be having at all levels. Even she does not know exactly what these processes of rebirth will manifest for her as far as her outer crust is concerned. There are some indications of where safe settlement might occur, which accounts for the information currently in print.

Secondly, the human beings residing on the planet must align with their inner essence of spirit, just as the Earth is doing. Once they have done so, they will receive ongoing guidance as to when and where they should go in order to live in a state of high well being. One of the results of the changes in the world to come will be the spiritual expansion of human capabilities. Learning how to access the inner wisdom of spirit will prove to be the greatest accomplishment human beings will gain in the times ahead.

So, look to the future with anticipation and optimism. Your ancestors inhabiting this planet had long awaited the coming era. Many cultures knew that The Great Awakening would arrive at this point in time, and so they wrote and sang about it down through the ages. They knew that the people of Earth would grow in spirit and stature, reflecting their Divine Creator in all ways. So give thanks and feel appreciation for the gift that you have been given of living during these times.

The time of chaos is fast approaching the Earth. The ancient Greeks understood and believed deeply in the beauty of chaos. They knew it to be a time of great power and creativity when the boundaries of different worlds overlapped for a brief but magical moment. It is a time pregnant with potentiality for new beginnings and a different way of being. Time-based human reality folds in on itself, allowing a new way of life to grow up in the unformed vibration of an emerging world.

So reflect on these words. To most people, fear and anxiety play a dominant role in their thoughts and emotions at the start of this new Millennium. They can scarcely see the wonder and beauty of this momentous time in which they live. The power and majesty surrounding the completion of three great cycles is not recognized in any way. Most individuals are caught up in the Dance of Materiality that has permeated life on Earth for so long.

But, all over the planet, there are individuals and small groups who really sense at a deep level within themselves the positive aspect of what is transpiring. They have a feeling of expectancy and optimism in the face of all that is unfolding. They know in a deep inner part of their being that everything is for the highest good and will lead to a time of peace and joy.

Therefore, they allocate much of their time and efforts to preparing for what is coming, even though they are not sure how it will manifest. They know that they must ready themselves in all areas of their lives, so they can ride the wave that is approaching to sweep them into the new age. They strengthen and refine their physical bodies, challenging the dictates of time in order to climb the mountain of life ever higher. They seek out deep healing techniques for their mind and emotions. And they participate in whatever draws them to higher levels of spiritual development.

It is particularly to these people all over the Earth that these writings are directed. We express our honor and appreciation for the fine work that you are doing. You are truly the pioneers for the coming times. Your courage and dedication is cheered by those beings like us on the realms of spirit who are assisting in the unfolding of the Divine Plan. Attune to us and join with us in this Great Step Forward in which we together are creating a new heaven and a new Earth. The entities in the many dimensions of the Creator are rejoicing. Can you not hear them? Feel their joy and radiate it out, so that it encircles the Earth in a band of light and love. For it carries the timeless message "We are all One dancing in the fields of the Holy Spirit to reach the Highest Good".

This ends our first series of transmissions.

We love you all.
The Lightbringers

www.ingramcontent.com/pod-product-compliance
Lightning Source LLC
LaVergne TN
LVHW051234080426
835513LV00016B/1589